Progress™
Mathematics

2

S Sadlier School

Cover: *Series Design:* Studio Montage; *Title design:* Quarasan, Inc. **Photo Credits:** Cover: age fotostock/Zoonar/N Sorokin: *right.* Getty Images/ Daryl Solomon: *top left.* Used under license from Shutterstock.com/RoboLab: *background.* Interior: Blend Images/Radius Images: 144 *top.* Corbis/Blend Images/JGI/Jamie Grill: 54 *top.* Dreamstime.com/Viktor Gladkov: vi *top right;* Oleg Zhukov: 145. Getty Images/Mark Bowden: 246 *top;* John Lund/Sam Diephuis: 9; SelectStock: 8 *top;* Daryl Solomon: vi *center.* iStockphoto.com/busypix: 55. Used under license from Shutter- stock.com/Cimpinski: 145 *inset;* elisekurenbina: vi *bottom left;* FocusDzign: vi *top left;* Jana Guothova: 8 *bottom,* 54 *bottom,* 144 *bottom,* 246 *bottom;* Ian 2010: vi *bottom right;* RoboLab: 1, vi *background.* **Text Credit:** Common Core State Standards Copyright © 2010. National Governors Association Center for Best Practices and Council of Chief State School Officers. All rights reserved. **Illustrator Credit:** Bob Holt

For additional online resources, go to sadlierconnect.com.

William H. Sadlier, Inc.
9 Pine Street
New York, NY 10005-4700

Printed in the United States of America.
ISBN: 978-1-4217-3152-0
1 2 3 4 5 6 7 8 9 WEBC 18 17 16 15 14

Contents

continued on next page

Unit 3   Focus on Measurement and Data

Unit 4 Focus on Geometry

Welcome

You have an exciting year ahead of you. You will be learning about mathematics and the tools you will need to solve problems.

Did you know that you solve problems and use math every day? When you play sports, go shopping, cook, build something, or travel in a car, bus or train, you are using math.

Progress Mathematics will help you improve your math skills. With it, you may even do better in school. That's why the book is called *Progress*.

Have a great year!

Progress Check

Look at how the math concepts and skills you have learned and will learn connect.

It is very important for you to understand the math concepts and skills from the prior grade level so that you will be able to develop an understanding of operations and algebraic thinking in this unit and be prepared for next year. To practice your skills, go to sadlierconnect.com.

Unit 1

GRADE 1	Before Unit 1	GRADE 2	After Unit 1	GRADE 3
I Can...		**Can I ?**		**I Will...**
Add or subtract within 20 to solve word problems	☐	Solve one- and two-step word problems by adding and subtracting within 100	☐	Solve two-step problems using the four operations
Use objects, drawings, and equations to represent word problems	☐	Use drawings and equations to represent word problems	☐	Use equations to represent word problems
Find the unknown number in an addition or subtraction equation				Solve word problems by adding and subtracting units of time
				Solve one-step problems by adding or subtracting units of mass or volume
Fluently add and subtract within 10	☐	Fluently add and subtract within 20	☐	Fluently add and subtract within 1,000
Add and subtract within 20				
	☐	Tell if a group of objects has an odd or even number of members	☐	Identify arithmetic patterns
	☐	Show an even number as the sum of two equal addends	☐	
	☐	Add to find the total number of objects in an array	☐	Understand products of whole numbers
				Fluently multiply and divide within 100

HOME CONNECT...

In this unit, your child will:

- Solve problems using addition and subtraction.

- Add and subtract within 100.

- Identify odd and even numbers.

- Write equations to show how many objects are in an array.

Ways to Help Your Child

Flash cards are a fun way for your child to practice addition and subtraction facts. You and your child can make a set of flash cards using index cards. Write one fact on the front of each card and write the answer on the back. Encourage your child to review the flash cards daily. Challenge your child to create a game using the flash cards.

In second grade, your child will need to know how to add and subtract within 100. Understanding the relationship between addition and subtraction is very important.

An array is a set of objects arranged in rows and columns. Your child will learn how to write equations to show how many objects are in an array.

Here is an example of an array.
In this array, there are 3 rows.
There are 2 in each row.
One equation for this array is
$2 + 2 + 2 = 6$.

Also in this array, there are 2 columns.
There are 3 in each column.

Another equation for this array is $3 + 3 = 6$.

Work with arrays will prepare your child for multiplication in Grade 3.

Activity: Your child will be asked to determine if a group of objects has an odd or even number of objects. Odd numbers end with 1, 3, 5, 7, or 9. Even numbers end with 0, 2, 4, 6, or 8. There are several strategies your child might use, such as make pairs of objects or skip-count by 2s. Ask your child if some of the numbers of objects encountered at home are odd or even. Then discuss the strategy he or she used to determine this.

ONLINE

For more Home Connect activities, continue online at sadlierconnect.com

Focus on Operations and Algebraic Thinking

Essential Question:
How can you solve addition and subtraction problems?

Problem Solving: Addition

Essential Question:
How can you use addition to solve word problems?

Words to Know
add
sum
equation
addend

Guided Instruction

In this lesson you will learn different ways to solve addition word problems.

Understand: Use drawings and equations to solve addition word problems

> There are 8 frogs sitting on a log.
> Then 11 more frogs jump onto the log.
> How many frogs are on the log in all?

You want to find how many frogs in all.
You need to add the numbers.

Draw a picture to help you find the sum.

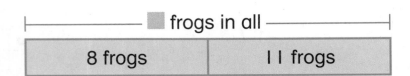

|— ⬛ frogs in all —|

8 frogs	11 frogs

Write an equation. An equation is a number sentence with an equal sign.

$$8 + 11 = \blacksquare$$

8 frogs and 11 more frogs is 19 frogs in all.

$$8 + 11 = 19$$

▷ There are 19 frogs in all.

Understand: Write an equation to solve an addition word problem

> Joanne has a sticker album. She has
> 15 baseball stickers and 20 football stickers.
> How many stickers does Joanne have
> in her album?

You are putting two groups together.

One group has 15 baseball stickers.
The other group has 20 football stickers.

Add to find how many stickers Joanne
has in her album.

Write an addition equation.
Use the numbers you know.
Use ■ for the number you do not know.

$$15 + 20 = \blacksquare$$

■ stickers in all
15 baseball stickers	20 football stickers

$$15 + 20 = \underline{35}$$

▷ Joanne has _____ stickers in her album.

Remember!
You can use a picture
to help find the sum.

Guided Instruction

Connect: Some word problems have more than one step

> Ted had 14 baseball cards and 2 football cards.
> Kate gave him more cards. Now Ted has 36 cards.
> How many cards did Kate give him?

Step 1

First find how many cards Ted had at the start.
Write an addition equation.

$14 + 2 = \blacksquare$

Start at 14. Count on 2. $14 \longrightarrow 15, 16$

$14 + 2 = \underline{16}$

Ted had _____ cards at the start.

Step 2

Next find how many cards Kate gave Ted.
Write an equation. You know Ted had 16 cards to start.
Now he has 36 cards.

$16 + \blacksquare = 36$

Add 10 to 16. $\longrightarrow$ $16 + 10 = 26$
Add 10 more. $\longrightarrow$ $26 + 10 = 36$

$16 + \underline{} = 36$

➡ Kate gave Ted _____ cards.

If Kate gave Ted 10 more cards, how many cards

would Ted have then? _____ cards

Guided Practice

1. **Ty has 17 horses. He has 40 more chickens than horses. How many chickens does he have?**

Step 1

You want to find how many chickens Ty has.

You know he has _____ horses. One addend is _____.

He has _____ more chickens than horses.

The other addend is _____.

Write an addition equation. _____ + _____ = ▇

Step 2

Model the problem. Then count on by 10s to add.

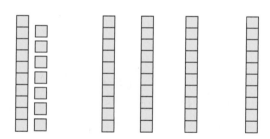

17 ⟶ 27, 37, _____, _____

17 + 40 = _____

Ty has _____ chickens.

 Think•Pair•Share

MP2 2. There are 12 cows and 5 roosters on the farm. Write an addition equation to find how many more cows there are than roosters. Tell how you found your answer.

Independent Practice

Draw a picture to model the problem. Write an addition equation. Then solve the problem.

1. There are 13 ducks in the pond. Then 7 more ducks come into the pond. How many ducks are in the pond now?

   _____ + _____ = _____

   There are _____ ducks in the pond now.

2. There are 28 flowers in the vase. Marta puts 3 more flowers into the vase. How many flowers are in the vase now?

   _____ + _____ = _____

   There are _____ flowers in the vase now.

3. Connor has 10 more toy cars than Aidan. Aidan has 14 toy cars. How many toy cars does Connor have?

   _____ + _____ = _____

   Connor has _____ toy cars.

4. Alana has 12 more baseball cards than Tina. Tina has 17 baseball cards. How many baseball cards does Alana have?

   _____ + _____ = _____

   Alana has _____ baseball cards.

Independent Practice

Circle the correct equation to solve each part of the problem. Then solve the problem.

5. There were 6 blueberry muffins and 11 corn muffins in a box. The baker put 7 more blueberry muffins into the box. How many muffins are there in the box in all?

   Find how many muffins at the start.

   $6 + 11 = 17$ $6 + 5 = 11$ $6 + 7 = 13$

   Find how many muffins in the box in all.

   $11 + 7 = 18$ $17 + 7 = 24$ $13 + 7 = 20$

   There are _____ muffins in the box in all.

Complete each equation to solve the problem.

6. There were 5 puzzles and 7 games in the toy box. Olga put 4 more puzzles into the box. How many puzzles and games are in the toy box now?

   Find how many puzzles and games in the box to start.

   _____ puzzles + _____ games = _____ in all

   Find how many puzzles and games in the box now.

   _____ + _____ = _____

   There are _____ puzzles and games in the toy box now.

Independent Practice

Write the addition equation you can use to solve the problem. Then solve the problem.

7. There are 15 oranges and some apples in a fruit basket. There are 24 oranges and apples in all in the basket. How many apples are in the basket?

_____ + ▪ = _____

There are _____ apples in the basket.

8. Brad has 15 shells in a bag. He adds more shells to the bag. Now there are 35 shells in the bag. How many shells did Brad add to the bag?

_____ + ▪ = _____

Brad added _____ shells to the bag.

9. Judy did some homework for 25 minutes. After dinner she did more homework for 20 minutes. How much time did Judy spend doing homework?

_____ + _____ = ▪

Judy spent _____ minutes doing homework.

10. Tara has 28 rocks in her collection. Juan has a rock collection too. Together Tara and Juan have 68 rocks. How many rocks does Juan have in his collection?

_____ + ▪ = _____

Juan has _____ rocks in his collection.

Independent Practice

Solve each problem.

11. There were some pennies in a jar. Irene put 40 more pennies into the jar. Then there were 82 pennies in the jar. How many pennies were in the jar at the start?

_____ + _____ = _____

There were _____ pennies in the jar at the start.

12. Kevin had 34 stamps in his collection. He bought 20 more stamps. Then his uncle gave him 3 more stamps. How many stamps does Kevin have in all?

_____ + _____ = _____

_____ + _____ = _____

Kevin has _____ stamps in all.

MP8 **13.** Mrs. Smith has 56 beads to put into two bags. She put some of the beads in a blue bag. She put 31 beads in a purple bag. How many beads did Mrs. Smith put in the blue bag?

Write an equation to show how many beads there are in the blue bag. Then solve the equation.

_____ + _____ = _____

Mrs. Smith put _____ beads in the blue bag.

Then Mrs. Smith bought more beads. She put all her new beads into the purple bag. She now has 71 beads in the purple bag. How many new beads did Mrs. Smith buy?

Tell how you found your answer.

Problem Solving: Subtraction

Essential Question:
How can you use subtraction to solve word problems?

Words to Know
subtract
difference

Guided Instruction

In this lesson you will learn different ways to solve subtraction word problems.

Understand: Use drawings and equations to solve subtraction word problems

> There were 17 birds in a tree. Some flew away. Now there are 7 birds. How many birds flew away?

You want to find how many birds flew away.

Now there are fewer birds than before, so you will subtract to find the answer.

Draw a picture. Start with 17 circles.
Cross out one at a time until 7 are left.
Count how many you cross out.

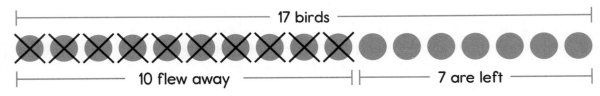

17 birds

10 flew away | 7 are left

Write a subtraction equation.

$$17 - \blacksquare = 7$$

birds in the tree at start | birds that flew away | birds in the tree now

$$17 - 10 = 7$$

The number being subtracted from 17 is 10.

▷ 10 birds flew away.

Guided Instruction

Understand: Use related addition and subtraction equations to solve a subtraction word problem

> There were some apples on a tray.
> Steve takes 20 apples. Then 18 apples are left.
> How many apples were on the tray at the start?

Make a drawing to show the problem.

■ apples on the tray at start	
20 apples that Steve takes	18 apples left

First write a subtraction equation. Use the numbers you know.

$$\blacksquare \quad - \quad 20 \quad = \quad 18$$

↑	↑	↑
apples on tray at start	apples that Steve takes	apples left

Use 18 and 20 to write a related addition equation. The 18 apples left and the 20 that Steve takes together equal the number of apples at the start.

$18 + 20 = \blacksquare$

Add: $18 + 20 = 38$

The sum, 38, was the missing number in the subtraction equation.

$38 - 20 = 18$

> **Remember!**
> Related addition and subtraction equations use the same numbers.

▷ There were 38 apples on the tray at the start.

Guided Instruction

Connect: Solve subtraction word problems that have two steps

Polly and Jeff are building a tower with blocks.
When the tower is 14 blocks tall, Polly takes
5 blocks off. Then Jeff puts 9 blocks on.
How many blocks are in the tower now?

Step 1

Find how many blocks are in the tower after Polly takes 5 off.

Write and solve an equation to find the **difference**.

$$14 - 5 = \blacksquare$$

↑ blocks at start   ↑ blocks Polly takes off   ↑ blocks left in tower

$$14 - 5 = \underline{9}$$

There are _____ 9 blocks in the tower after Polly takes 5 off.

Step 2

Find how many blocks are in the tower after Jeff puts 9 on.

Write and solve an equation.

$$9 + 9 = \blacksquare$$

↑ blocks left in tower   ↑ blocks Jeff puts on   ↑ blocks in tower now

$$9 + 9 = \underline{18}$$

▷ There are _____ 18 blocks in the tower now.

Guided Practice

1. A theater has 45 seats. The people who came to see the show are seated. There are 10 empty seats. How many people are seated?

Step 1

Draw a picture to model the problem. Show 45 seats. Cross off 10 to stand for the empty seats.

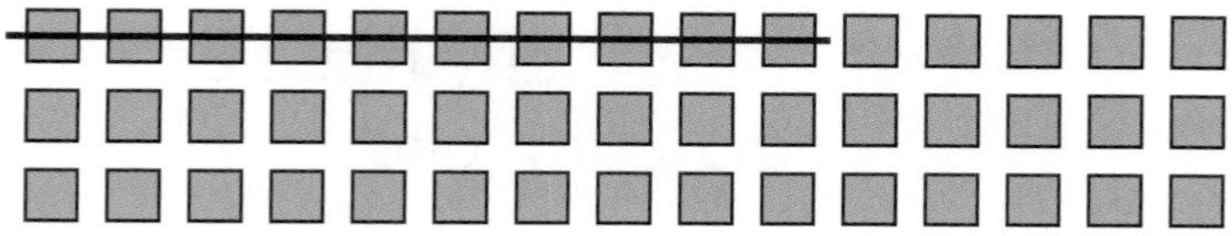

Step 2

How many seats are there in all? 45

How many empty seats are there? _____

Write a subtraction equation to help you find how many people are seated.

_____ − _____ = ■ 45 − 10 = _____

There are _____ people seated.

Think•Pair•Share

MP1 2. Brandon has 30 fewer baseball cards than Luke. Luke has 7 more baseball cards than Margaret. Margaret has 89 baseball cards.

How many baseball cards does Brandon have? _____

Talk about how you found your answer.

Independent Practice

**Draw a picture to model the problem.
Write a subtraction equation.
Then solve the problem.**

1. There were 19 bananas.
   Ernie takes 13.
   How many bananas
   are left?

   _____ – _____ = _____

   There are _____
   bananas left.

2. There were 22 marbles
   in a jar. Lara took some
   marbles. Then 12 marbles
   were left in the jar.
   How many marbles
   did Lara take?

   _____ – _____ = _____

   Lara took _____ marbles.

3. There are 35 flowers
   in a vase. 10 are white
   and the rest are red.
   How many flowers
   are red?

   _____ – _____ = _____

   There are _____ red flowers.

4. Ryan has 30 fewer
   counters than Sam.
   Sam has 48 counters.
   How many counters
   does Ryan have?

   _____ – _____ = _____

   Ryan has _____ counters.

Complete each equation to solve the problem.

5. There were 13 children at the playground.
   Then 5 children left to go home for lunch,
   and 4 children left to go to the lunchroom.
   How many children are at the playground now?

   Find how many children left the playground.

   _____ + _____ = _____

   Find how many children did not leave
   the playground.

   _____ − _____ = _____

   How many children are at the playground now?

   _____

6. One morning Angelo made 45 pizzas in his shop.
   He sold 14 pizzas at lunchtime. Then he sold 6 more
   after lunch. How many pizzas were left over?

   Find how many pizzas Angelo sold in all.

   _____ + _____ = _____

   Find how many pizzas were left over.

   _____ − _____ = _____

   How many pizzas were left over?

   _____

Independent Practice

Circle the correct equation to solve the problem.

7. Larry has 24 stickers. Rita has 13 stickers.
How many fewer stickers does Rita have
than Larry?

$$24 - 13 = 11 \qquad 24 + 13 = 37 \qquad 37 - 13 = 24$$

8. Jacob has 21 fewer pennies than Connor.
Connor has 47 pennies. How many pennies
does Jacob have?

$$47 + 21 = 68 \qquad 47 - 21 = 26 \qquad 68 - 21 = 47$$

**Write a related addition equation to help
solve the problem.**

9. There were 39 cows eating
together in a field. Some
walked away. Now there
are 19 cows eating
together. How many cows
walked away?

$$39 - \blacksquare = 19$$

related equation:

____ + ____ = ____

____ cows walked away.

10. There were 53 cars parked
in a lot. Now there are
23 cars in the lot. How many
cars were moved out
of the lot?

$$53 - \blacksquare = 23$$

related equation:

____ + ____ = ____

____ cars were moved out.

Independent Practice

MP4 **11.** Amanda had saved some quarters.
She used 30 quarters.
Then she had 12 quarters left.
How many quarters did Amanda have at the start?
Explain how you solved the problem
and make a drawing to model the problem.

_____

MP2 **12.** Travis rides his bike 20 fewer miles than Jonah.
Travis rides 9 miles in all. Jonah rides 10 miles
and then stops for a snack. After his snack,
Jonah gets back on his bike and rides some more.
How many miles did Jonah ride after his snack?
Explain how you solved the problem.

_____

Essential Question:
What strategies can you use to add and subtract?

Guided Instruction

In this lesson you will learn different ways to add and subtract.

Understand: Make a ten to help you add

Lisa has 8 blue buttons. Ryan has 7 red buttons. How many buttons do they have in all?

Write an equation for the problem.

$$8 + 7 = \blacksquare$$

Remember!
When you count on 2 from 8, say, "9, 10."

Use 8 blue counters and 7 red counters to model the problem. Then move 2 of the red ones to make a ten.

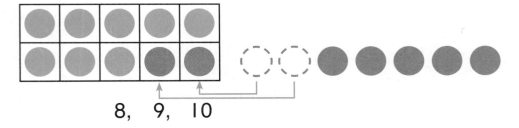

8, 9, 10

Add the red counters that are left to the 10.

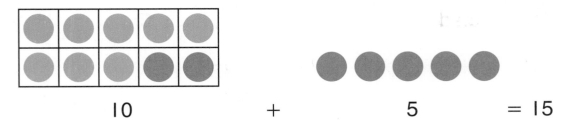

10 $+$ 5 $=$ 15

$10 + 5 = 15$, so $8 + 7 = 15$

▷ Lisa and Ryan have 15 buttons in all.

Guided Instruction

Understand: **Make a ten to help you subtract**

There were 15 cars parked. 8 cars were moved out. How many cars are left?

Write an equation for the problem. $15 - 8 = \blacksquare$

Step 1

Make a ten to help you subtract.

$8 = \underline{\hspace{1cm}} + \underline{\hspace{1cm}}$ so $15 - 8$ is like $15 - \underline{\hspace{1cm}} - \underline{\hspace{1cm}}$.

To make a ten, subtract $\underline{\hspace{1cm}}$ from 15. $15 - 5 = \underline{\hspace{1cm}}$.

Step 2

Now subtract 3. $\longrightarrow$ $10 - 3 = \underline{\hspace{1cm}}$

$15 - 5 - 3 = 7$, so $15 - 8 = 7$

▷ There are 7 cars left.

Understand: **Addition and subtraction are related**

Use a related addition fact to find $15 - 8 = \blacksquare$.

The sum in the related addition fact is 15.
An addend in the related addition fact is 8.

$8 + \underline{\hspace{1cm}} = 15$

$8 + 7 = 15$ and $15 - 8 = 7$ are related facts.

▷ $15 - 8 = 7$

Remember!
Related facts use the same numbers.

Guided Instruction

Connect: **Use related facts to help you add and subtract**

$$14 - 9 = \blacksquare$$

Step 1

Use the two numbers you know to write a related addition fact.

Which number will be the sum? _14_

Which number will be an addend? _9_

_9_ + $\blacksquare$ = _14_

Step 2

What is the missing addend in $9 + \blacksquare = 14$?

Make a ten.   9 and how many more is 10? _____

$9 + 1 = 10$.   10 and how many more is 14? _____

You added _____ to make 10.

Then you added _____ to make 14.

_____ + _____ = 5, so the missing addend is 5.

$9 + 5 = 14$

Step 3

Use the related addition fact to write the subtraction fact.

$9 + 5 = 14$ and $14 - 9 = 5$ are related facts.

▷ $14 - 9 = 5$

Guided Practice

I. **Use a related fact to subtract 11 − 7 = ▇.**

Step 1

Use the two numbers you know to write a related addition fact.

Which number should you write as the sum? _____

Which number should you write as an addend? _____

Write the numbers you know for the related addition fact.

_____ + ▇ = _____

Step 2

Make a ten.   7 and how many more is 10? _____

$7 + 3 = 10$ 10 and how many more is 11? _____

You added _____ to make 10, and _____ more to make 11.

The missing addend is _____. $7 + 4 = 11$

Step 3

Use the related addition fact to write the subtraction fact.

$7 + 4 = 11$ and $11 − 7 =$ _____

$11 − 7 =$ _____

 **Think•Pair•Share**

MP3   2. Show two ways to find $14 − 8 = ▇$.

Talk about your work.

Independent Practice

Complete each addition or subtraction fact.
Use the pictures to help you.

1. 8 + 9 = 17

2. 18 − 9 = 9

3. 13 − 4 = 9

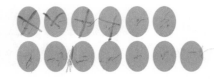

4. 8 + 6 = 14

5. 5 + 6 = 11

6. 12 − 5 = 7

7. 6 + 7 = 13

8. 15 − 7 = 8

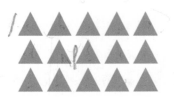

Independent Practice

MP3 35. You want to find the missing number in $12 - 8 = $ ▮.
Show two ways to do this. Explain your thinking.

> One way

> Another way

MP3 36. Robert says that the facts below are **all** related facts
for $13 - 9 = 4$.

$$13 + 9 = 22 \qquad 9 + 4 = 13 \qquad 13 + 4 = 17$$
$$13 - 4 = 9 \qquad 4 + 9 = 13$$

Is he correct? _____

Why or why not? Explain.

Essential Question:
How can you tell if a number is odd or even?

Words to Know
even number
odd number

Guided Instruction

In this lesson you will learn about odd numbers and even numbers.

Understand: Even numbers of objects make pairs

Rich has 8 toy cars. Does he have an odd number or an even number of toy cars?

Start with 8 toy cars.

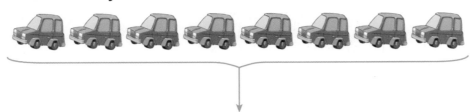

Make pairs. Are there any left over?

2   4   6   8

There are four pairs of toy cars.
No toy cars are left over.
8 is an even number.

Remember!
A pair is a group of 2 objects.

An even number has the digit 0, 2, 4, 6, or 8 in the ones place.

▷ Rich has an even number of toy cars.

Understand: Odd numbers of objects make pairs with 1 left over

Tania has 7 apples. Does she have an odd number or an even number of apples?

Start with 7 apples. Make pairs. Are there any left over?

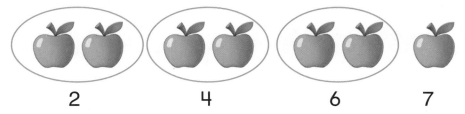

2   4   6   7

There are 3 pairs with 1 left over.

7 is an odd number.

An odd number has the digit 1, 3, 5, 7, or 9 in the ones place.

▷ Tania has an odd number of apples.

Understand: Skip-count by 2s to tell if a number is even or odd

How many flowers? Is that number odd or even?

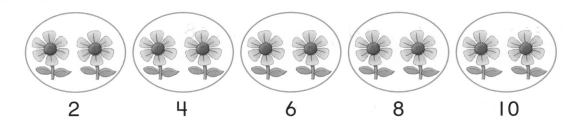

2   4   6   8   10

▷ There are 10 flowers. The number 10 is an even number.

Guided Instruction

Connect: You can write an equation to show that even numbers make two equal groups

How can you put 4 basketballs into two equal groups?

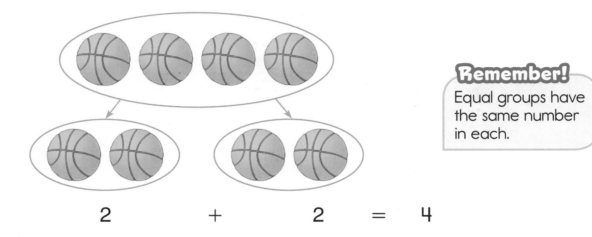

Remember!
Equal groups have the same number in each.

$$2 \quad + \quad 2 \quad = \quad 4$$

▷ A group of 4 can make two groups of 2.

How can you put 6 fish into two equal groups?

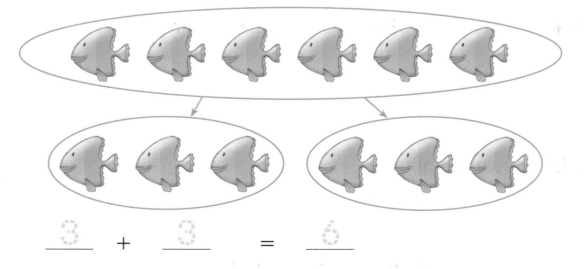

$$\underline{3} \quad + \quad \underline{3} \quad = \quad \underline{6}$$

▷ There are ____ fish in each group.

1. **Which number is even, 13 or 16? Draw equal groups and write an equation to show how you know.**

Step 1

Show 13 and 16 with pictures. Try to make two equal groups for each number.

Can you make two equal groups from 13? _____

Can you make two equal groups from 16? _____

When you add equal groups the sum is an even number.

Step 2

Write an equation for each picture above.

$6 + 7 = 13$ 13 is an _____ number.

$8 + 8 = 16$ 16 is an _____ number.

You can always use doubles to write an addition equation for an even number.

_____ is an even number.

 **Think•Pair•Share**

MP3 **2.** Rita says that 19 is an odd number. Sally says 19 is an even number. Who is correct? Explain why.

Independent Practice

Circle pairs of objects. Then tell if the number is even or odd.

1.

7 is an _____ number.

2.

10 is an _____ number.

3.

4 is an _____ number.

4.

5 is an _____ number.

5.

14 is an _____ number.

6.

11 is an _____ number.

Circle the correct answer.

7. Which shows an odd number of turtles?

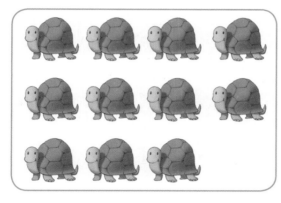 

11   10

8. Which shows an odd number of kites?

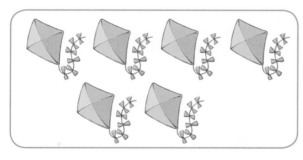 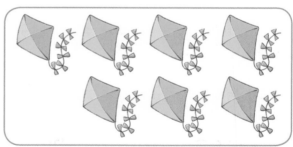

6   7

9. Which shows an even number of flowers?

12   13

Independent Practice

Circle the correct answers.

10. Circle all the odd numbers.

14   16   17   18   19

11. Circle all the even numbers.

2   4   7   9   10

12. Circle all the even numbers.

11   15   16   18   20

13. Circle all the odd numbers.

8   9   11   12   14

Write true or false.

14. 12 is an odd number. _____

15. 16 is an even number. _____

16. 15 and 19 are both odd numbers. _____

Complete the sentences. Write *even* or *odd*.

17. 22 is an _____ number.

18. 35 is an _____ number.

19. 13 is an _____ number.

20. 28 is an _____ number.

Independent Practice

21. Fill in the missing numbers to show that 14 is an even number.

_____ + _____ = 14

22. Fill in the missing numbers to show that 17 is an odd number.

_____ + _____ + _____ = 17

MP1 23. Henry writes 15 on the board. He says that 15 is an odd number. Draw a picture to show if he is correct. Talk about your answer.

MP2 24. Look at the numbers below. Find the even number. Use equal groups to prove you are correct. Then write an addition equation to check your work.

22   21   19

5 Arrays

Essential Question:
How can you find how many objects are in an array?

Words to Know
  array

Guided Instruction

In this lesson you will learn how to write equations to show how many in an array.

Understand: Use repeated addition to find how many in all

Rosie put some red apples into a box.
There are 3 rows of apples in the box.
There are 4 apples in each row.
How many apples in all are in the box?

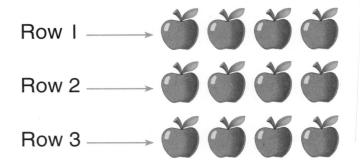

Row 1 ⟶

Row 2 ⟶

Row 3 ⟶

There are 4 apples in Row 1.
There are 4 apples in Row 2.
There are 4 apples in Row 3.

Write an equation to find how many apples in all.
You can add to find how many in all.

$$4 + 4 + 4 = 12$$

▷ There are 12 apples in all.

Guided Instruction

Understand: You arrange things in equal rows and equal columns to make an array

Look at the rows. Write an equation for the array.

Row 1	● ● ●	→	3
Row 2	● ● ●	→	3
Row 3	● ● ●	→	3
Row 4	● ● ●	→	3

The array has 4 rows with 3 counters in each row.

▷ $3 + 3 + 3 + 3 = \underline{12}$

Now look at the columns. Write an equation for the array.

Columns ⟶ 1   2   3

● ● ●
● ● ●
● ● ●
● ● ●
↓ ↓ ↓
4   4   4

The array has 3 columns with 4 counters in each column.

▷ $4 + 4 + 4 = \underline{12}$

Guided Instruction

Connect: Different arrays can show the same number

> Sandy and Ralph have the same number of counters.
> They each used all their counters to make an array.
> Do both arrays show the same number?

Look at Sandy's rows and columns.
There are 2 rows. There are 4 in each row.
Write an equation to find how many in all.

$$4 + 4 = \underline{8}$$

Sandy's array

There are 4 columns. There are 2 in
each column. Write an equation to find
how many in all.

$$2 + 2 + 2 + 2 = \underline{8}$$

Look at Ralph's rows and columns.

How many rows? ___4___

How many in each row? ___2___

Write an equation to find how many in all.

$$\underline{2} + \underline{2} + \underline{2} + \underline{2} = \underline{8}$$

How many columns? ___2___

How many in each column? ___4___

Ralph's array

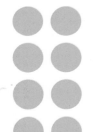

Write an equation to find how many in all.

$$\underline{4} + \underline{4} = \underline{8}$$

Compare the equations.

▷ Both arrays show the same number, 8.

1. **Write two equations for this array.**

Step 1

Look at the rows.

There are ___2___ rows. There are ___6___ in each row.

Write one equation.

___ + ___ = ___

Step 2

Look at the columns.

There are ___6___ columns. There are ___2___ in each column.

Write another equation.

___ + ___ + ___ + ___ + ___ + ___ = ___

The two equations for the array are

___ + ___ = ___ and ___ + ___ + ___ + ___ + ___ + ___ = ___

Think·Pair·Share

MP8　2. Draw a different array for 12. Write two equations for your array. Then compare the array above to your array. Talk about how the arrays are alike and how they are different.

Independent Practice

Look at the arrays. Write how many rows and columns.

1.
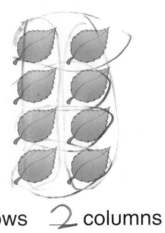
4 rows   2 columns

2.

2 rows   2 columns

3.
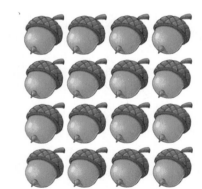
4 rows   4 columns

4.

3 rows   4 columns

5.

3 rows   5 columns

6.

3 rows   3 columns

Circle the two arrays that show the same number.

7.

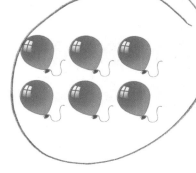  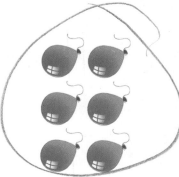

8.

 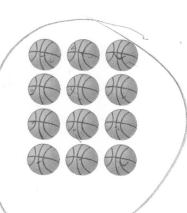 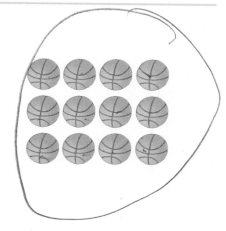

9.

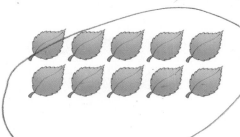 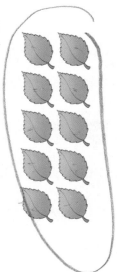 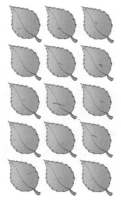

Independent Practice

Write two equations for each array.

10.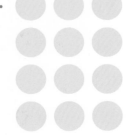

___ + ___ + ___ + ___ = ___

___ + ___ + ___ = ___

11.

___ + ___ = ___

___ + ___ + ___ + ___ + ___ = ___

12.

___ + ___ + ___ = ___

___ + ___ = ___

13.

___ + ___ = ___

___ + ___ + ___ + ___ = ___

14. Circle the equations for this array.

$3 + 3 + 3 + 3 + 3 = 15$

$4 + 4 + 4 = 12$

$5 + 5 + 5 = 15$

$3 + 3 + 3 + 3 = 12$

Independent Practice

MP3 **15.** Mrs. Bennett drew these arrays. Tommy thinks they show the same number. Connor does not. Who is correct? Explain your answer using equations.

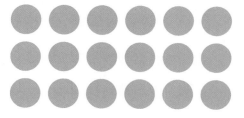 

MP4 **16.** Draw an array with 4 rows and 5 counters in each row. Write two equations for the array.

Draw a different array to show 20. Use 2 rows. Write two equations for the array.

Write a related subtraction fact.

1. $8 + 6 = 14$

   ___ – ___ = ___

2. $4 + 9 = 13$

   ___ – ___ = ___

Circle the correct answers.

3. Circle all the even numbers.

   12   13   15   17   18

4. Circle all the odd numbers.

   4   6   7   8   9

Add or subtract.

5. $16 - 9 =$ ___

6. $8 +$ ___ $= 11$

7. ___ $- 5 = 8$

8. ___ $+ 9 = 17$

9. $15 - 6 =$ ___

10. $14 -$ ___ $= 7$

11. ___ $+ 8 = 15$

12. $9 + 9 =$ ___

13. Circle the correct equation to solve the problem.

    Brady has 32 fewer marbles than Emma.
    Emma has 63 marbles.
    How many marbles does Brady have?

    $63 + 32 = 95$ $63 - 32 = 31$ $95 - 32 = 63$

14. Draw a picture to model the problem.
    Write a subtraction equation. Then solve the problem.

    There were 29 acorns.
    Molly took some of them.
    Now there are 14 acorns.
    How many acorns did Molly take?

    _____ − _____ = _____

    Molly took _____ acorns.

Write and solve an addition equation to solve the problem.

15. Antonio collects 16 pinecones on Friday and 20 on Saturday. How many pinecones does he collect in all?

    _____ + _____ = ▪

    Antonio collects _____ pinecones in all.

16. Noah has 19 shells. Gia has some shells too. Together Noah and Gia have 31 shells. How many shells does Gia have?

    _____ + ▪ = _____

    Gia has _____ shells.

MP2 **17.** Circle the even number. Draw 2 equal groups to check that you are correct. Then write an addition equation to show your work.

          11   10   9

____ + ____ = ____

18. Look at the rows. Complete the equation to tell how many hearts in all.

$4 + 4 + 4 = $ ____

19. Look at the array. Circle the equation that shows how many flowers.

$5 + 5 + 5 = 15$

$4 + 4 + 4 + 4 = 16$

$5 + 5 + 5 + 5 = 20$

MP4 **20.** Draw an array with 2 rows and 3 counters in each row. Write two equations for the array. Tell what each equation shows.

Progress Check

Look at how the math concepts and skills you have learned and will learn connect.

It is very important for you to understand the math concepts and skills from the prior grade level so that you will be able to develop an understanding of number and operations in base ten in this unit and be prepared for next year. To practice your skills, go to sadlierconnect.com.

GRADE 1	Before Unit 2	GRADE 2	After Unit 2	GRADE 3
I Can...		**Can I ?**		**I Will...**
Understand place value in two-digit numbers as tens and ones	☐	Understand place value in three-digit numbers as hundreds, tens, and ones	☐	Round whole numbers to the nearest 10 or 100
Understand 10 as ten ones	☐	Understand 100 as ten tens	☐	
Count to 120	☐	Count within 1,000	☐	
	☐	Skip-count by 5s, 10s, and 100s	☐	
	☐	Read and write numbers to 1,000	☐	
Compare two 2-digit numbers	☐	Compare two 3-digit numbers	☐	
Add within 100 / Subtract tens from tens	☐	Add and subtract within 100	☐	Fluently add and subtract within 1,000
Solve word problems by adding three numbers	☐	Add up to four 2-digit numbers	☐	
Subtract tens from tens	☐	Add and subtract within 1,000	☐	Fluently add and subtract within 1,000
Mentally find 10 more or 10 less than a number from 10 to 90	☐	Mentally find 100 more or 100 less than a number from 100 to 900	☐	
	☐	Explain why addition and subtraction strategies work	☐	

In this unit, your child will:

- Understand hundreds, tens, and ones in place value.

- Skip-count by 5s, 10s, and 100s.

- Read and write numbers to 1,000.

- Compare numbers.

- Add and subtract two-digit numbers and three-digit numbers within 1,000.

- Add more than two numbers.

- Mentally add or subtract 10 or 100.

Your child will learn about the value of digits in a number, called place value. Your child will learn that 10 ones is equal to 1 ten and that 10 tens is equal to 100 ones, or 1 hundred. Your child will write numbers in a place-value chart to show how many hundreds, tens, and ones are in a three-digit number.

hundreds	tens	ones
1	5	7

The **1** in **157** is in the hundreds place. It has a value of 1 hundred, or 100.
The **5** in **157** is in the tens place. It has a value of 5 tens, or 50.
The **7** in **157** is in the ones place. It has a value of 7 ones, or 7.
157 has 1 hundred, 5 tens, and 7 ones.

Your child will learn to skip-count by 5s, 10s, and 100s.

Ways to Help Your Child

If your child needs help or excels at math you might talk to your child's math teacher. He or she will be able to suggest opportunities to work with your child to keep your child engaged.

Activity: Write a number from 0 to 9 on index cards—one number on a card. Give your child three cards and ask your child to arrange the cards to make a three-digit number. Have your child tell the number of hundreds, tens, and ones in the number he or she made.

You might ask your child to arrange the cards in the order that creates the greatest number. Then ask your child to arrange them in the order that creates the least number. As a bonus, ask your child to find the difference between the greatest number and the least number!

ONLINE

For more Home Connect activities, continue online at sadlierconnect.com

Focus on Number and Operations in Base Ten

Essential Question:
How does place value help you add and subtract?

Place Value: Hundreds, Tens, and Ones

Essential Question:
How do you find the value of each digit in a 3-digit number?

Words to Know
place-value chart
digits

Guided Instruction

In this lesson you will learn about place value in 3-digit numbers using hundreds, tens, and ones.

Understand: Models can show that 10 tens is the same as 1 hundred

This is 1 ten. ⟶ ▭▭▭▭▭▭▭
It is made up of 10 ones.
How can you group tens to make 1 hundred?

Put 10 tens together. The new model has 100 ones.

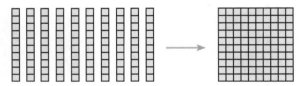

▷ The models show that 10 tens is the same as 1 hundred.

Understand: A place-value chart shows the value of each digit in a number

What does this place-value chart show?

hundreds	tens	ones
1	2	0

Digits are used to show numbers.
The digits are 0, 1, 2, 3, 4, 5, 6, 7, 8, 9.

▷ The place-value chart shows that the number 120 has 1 hundred, 2 tens, and 0 ones.

Connect: Use what you know to find the value of each digit in a number

Ella uses place-value blocks to show the number 243. What is the value of each digit in 243?

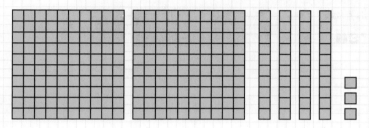

Step 1

Write how many hundreds, tens, and ones.

How many hundreds? There are ___2___ hundreds.

How many tens? There are ___4___ tens.

How many ones? There are ___3___ ones.

Step 2

Use the place-value chart to show the value of each digit in 243.

hundreds	tens	ones
2	4	3

The 2 in 243 stands for ___ hundreds.

The 4 in 243 stands for ___ tens.

The 3 in 243 stands for ___ ones.

Guided Practice

I. **What number do the place-value models show? What is the value of each digit in that number?**

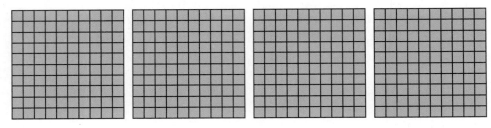

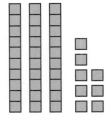

....

Step 1

Find the numbers of hundreds, tens, and ones.

How many hundreds? _____ hundreds

How many tens? _____ tens

How many ones? _____ ones

The number is _____.

....

Step 2

Use the place-value chart to show the value of each digit.

hundreds	tens	ones
4	3	8

The _____ stands for _____ hundreds.

The _____ stands for _____ tens.

The _____ stands for _____ ones.

2. **What number do these place-value models show?**

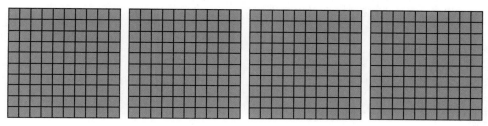

Step 1

Count the numbers of hundreds, tens, and ones.

How many hundreds are there? _____

How many tens are there? _____

How many ones are there? _____

Step 2

Use a place-value chart to show the value of each digit.

hundreds	tens	ones
4	0	0

4 hundreds 0 tens 0 ones is the same as _____.

The place-value models show _____.

 **Think•Pair•Share**

MP3 3. Which digit in 349 stands for the greatest value?
Tania says it is the 9. Otto says it is the 3.
Who is correct? Explain why.

Independent Practice

**Write how many hundreds, tens, and ones.
Then write the number.**

I.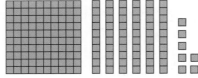

_____ hundred   _____ tens   _____ ones   _____

2.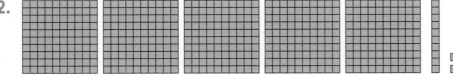

_____ hundreds   _____ ten   _____ ones   _____

3.

_____ hundreds   _____ tens   _____ ones   _____

4.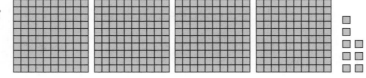

_____ hundreds   _____ tens   _____ ones   _____

Independent Practice

Circle the number that the place-value models show.

5.

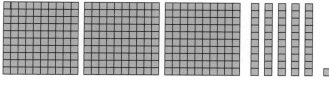

| 531 | 351 | 315 |

6.

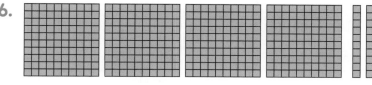

| 240 | 402 | 420 |

Circle the correct answer.

7. How many hundreds are in 630?

3   6   0

8. How many ones are in 236?

6   3   2

9. How many tens are in 824?

8   4   2

10. How many hundreds are in 195?

5   9   1

Independent Practice

11. What is the value of the 9 in 893? _____

12. What is the value of the 3 in 403? _____

13. What is the value of the 0 in 508? _____

14. What is the value of the 7 in 745? _____

15. What is the value of the 0 in 310? _____

16. What number has 4 hundreds 5 tens 0 ones? _____

17. What number has 5 hundreds 3 tens 1 one? _____

18. What number has 2 hundreds 2 tens 6 ones? _____

19. What number has 3 hundreds 7 tens 2 ones? _____

20. What number has 8 hundreds 0 tens 4 ones? _____

Independent Practice

MP4 **21.** Mr. Jones wrote 742 on the board. He asked the class to show the number with place-value models. Marta used the models below. Do Marta's models show the correct number? What might she have done wrong? Talk about it with a partner.

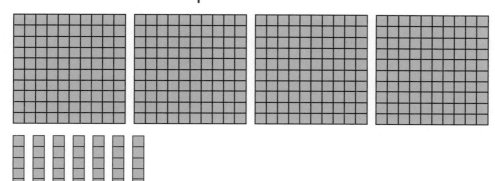

MP3 **22.** Use the digits 4, 5, and 2 to write three different 3-digit numbers. Tell what each digit in each number stands for.

7 Skip-Count by 5s, 10s, and 100s

Essential Question:
How can you count by 5s, 10s, and 100s?

Words to Know
skip-count

Guided Instruction

In this lesson you will learn to skip-count by 5s, 10s, and 100s.

Understand: Skip-counting by 5s

> Justine has 6 groups of 5 pennies.
> When she skip-counts the pennies by 5s,
> what numbers does she say?
> How many pennies does she have in all?

Skip-counting is counting by a number other than 1.
These counters are in 6 groups of 5.
Justine skip-counts them by 5s.

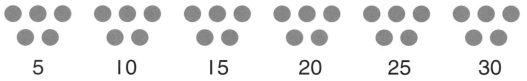

| 5 | 10 | 15 | 20 | 25 | 30 |

The last number Justine counts tells how many in all.
The blue boxes in this number chart show
skip-counting by 5s.

1	2	3	4	5	6	7	8	9	10
11	12	13	14	15	16	17	18	19	20
21	22	23	24	25	26	27	28	29	30

▷ When Justine counts her pennies, she says
the numbers 5, 10, 15, 20, 25, 30. She has
30 pennies in all.

Guided Instruction

Understand: Skip-counting by 10s

What numbers do you say when you skip-count by 10s to 100?

A number chart can help you skip-count.

1	2	3	4	5	6	7	8	9	10
11	12	13	14	15	16	17	18	19	20
21	22	23	24	25	26	27	28	29	30
31	32	33	34	35	36	37	38	39	40
41	42	43	44	45	46	47	48	49	50
51	52	53	54	55	56	57	58	59	60
61	62	63	64	65	66	67	68	69	70
71	72	73	74	75	76	77	78	79	80
81	82	83	84	85	86	87	88	89	90
91	92	93	94	95	96	97	98	99	100

Remember!
Patterns can help you count.

Look for a pattern in the number chart. The numbers in the blue boxes show skip-counting by 10s. Each number is 10 more than the number just above it.

Skip-count the models by 10s.

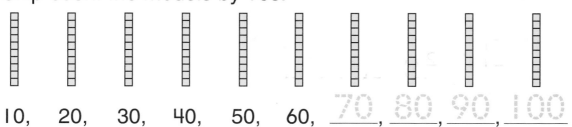

10,   20,   30,   40,   50,   60,   70, 80, 90, 100

When you skip-count by 10s to 100, say:

10, 20, 30, 40, 50, 60, _____, _____, _____, _____.

Guided Instruction

**Connect: What you know about skip-counting
to skip-count by 100s**

When Pat skip-counted by 100s to 700, she said
100, 200, 300, 400, ■, 600, 700.
What number did Pat miss saying?

Use hundreds models to show 700.
Start at 100. Skip-count by 100s to 700.
Look for a pattern to help find the missing number.

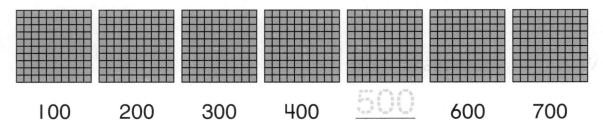

| 100 | 200 | 300 | 400 | _500_ | 600 | 700 |

Skip-count: _100_, _200_, _300_, _400_, _500_, _600_, _700_

When you count by 100s, the digit in the _hundreds_
place changes. The digits in the tens and ones places
stay the same.

▷ Pat missed saying _500_.

You can start at any number and still find a pattern.
Start at 140. Skip-count by 100s to 940.
What pattern do you see?

140, 240, 340, 440, 540, _640_, _740_, 840, _940_

Do the digits in the hundreds place stay the same? _____

Do the digits in the tens and ones places stay the same? _____

1. **What are the missing numbers?**

   5, 10, 15, 20, ▓, 30, ▓, ▓

Step 1

Look for a pattern to find the first missing number.

The pattern shows skip-counting by what number? __5__

When you skip-count by 5, the ones digit is __0__ or ____.

What number comes before the first missing number? ____

The ones digit in the first missing number is ____.

What is the first missing number? ____

Step 2

Use the pattern to find the other missing numbers.

What is the ones digit in the missing number

that comes next after 30? ____

What is that missing number? ____

What is the last missing number? ____

The missing numbers are ____, ____, and ____.

☆ Think•Pair•Share

MP3 2. Lucy is number 114 in a line for a museum. Bill is 10 people behind Lucy in the line. Erica is 10 people behind Bill. What number is Erica? Talk about how you know.

   Erica is number ____ in the line.

Independent Practice

Skip-count.

1.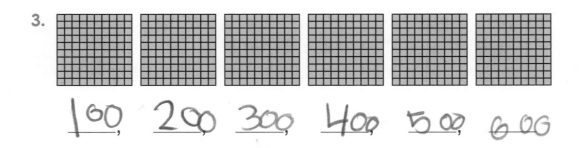

   10,   20,   30,   40

2.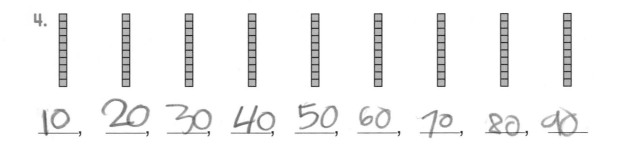

   5,   10,   15,   20,   25

3.

   1 00, 2 00 300, 4 00 5 00, 6 00

4.

   10, 20 30, 40, 50, 60, 70, 80, 90

Independent Practice

Write the missing numbers.

5. Skip-count by 5s.   5, 10, 15, 20, 25, 30, 35

6. Skip-count by 100s.   100, 200, 300, 400, 500, 600

7. Skip-count by 10s.   10, 20, 30, 40, 50, 60, 70

Circle the correct answer.

8. Linda skip-counted like this:
   100, 110, 120, 130, 140, 150, 160
   How did she skip-count?

   by 5s   (by 10s)   by 100s

9. Theo started at 300. He
   skip-counted by 100s.
   Which shows how
   Theo counted?

   300, 400, 500, 600, 700

   100, 200, 300, 400, 500

   300, 310, 320, 330, 340

10. See how Mia skip-counted.

    5, 10, 15, 20, 25, 30,

    What was the last number
    she said?

    40

    (35)

    45

Independent Practice

11. Skip-count by 100s.

250, 350, 450, _____, 650, _____ , 850, _____

12. Skip-count by 10s.

140, 150, 160, _____, 180, _____, _____, 210, _____, _____

13. Skip-count by 5s.

100, _____, 110, 115, _____, 125, 130, _____, _____, 145, _____

14. Skip-count by 100s.

176, 276, _____, 476, _____, _____, 776, _____, _____

15. Skip-count by 10s.

335, _____, _____, 365, _____, _____, 395, _____

16. Skip-count by 5s.

580, _____, _____, 595, _____, _____, 610, 615, _____

17. Skip-count by 5s.

470, _____, _____, 485, _____, 495, _____, _____, 510

Independent Practice

18. Skip-count by 10s.

380, _____, _____, 410, _____, _____, 440, 450, _____

Count by 1s to find the missing numbers.

19.

788	789			792	793	
		797	798			
	803	804		806		

20.

612			615		617	
		621	622	623		
626	627		629			

21. Suppose you are counting by 1s. What are the next five numbers that come just after 347?

347, _____, _____, _____, _____, _____

MP3 22. Rita skip-counted: 215, 225, 235, 245, 255, 265, 275.
She says she started at 215 and skip-counted by 5s.
Thomas says she skip-counted by 10s.
Who is right? Explain.

Read and Write Numbers to 1,000

Essential Question:
What are some ways to read and write numbers?

Words to Know
expanded form

Guided Instruction

In this lesson you will learn ways to read and write numbers to 1,000.

Understand: Place-value models can help you read and write numbers

Uma shows a number using place-value models.
What number do the models show?
Write the number, the number name, and the expanded form of the number.

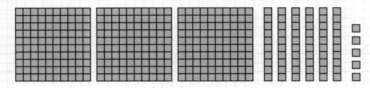

The models show 3 hundreds, 6 tens, 5 ones.

Write the number: 3 6 5

Write and read the number name: three hundred sixty-five.

Write the number 365 in expanded form. Use the value of each digit as an addend. Start with the hundreds.
   The 3 stands for 3 hundreds, or 300.
   The 6 stands for 6 tens, or 60.
   The 5 stands for 5 ones, or 5.

The addition 300 + 60 + 5 shows 365 in expanded form.

▷ The number is 365.
   The number name is three hundred sixty-five.
   The expanded form is 300 + 60 + 5.

Connect: A place-value chart can help you read and write numbers

What number does the place-value chart show?

hundreds	tens	ones
5	4	6

Write the number, the number name, and the expanded form.

The place-value chart shows that there are

5 hundreds, 4 tens, and 6 ones.

Use digits to write the number.

5 hundreds, 4 tens, 6 ones is the same as 546.

Write the number name.

five hundred forty-six

Write the number in expanded form.

The value of the digit in the hundreds place is 500.

The value of the digit in the tens place is 40.

The value of the digit in the ones place is 6.

The expanded form of 546 is 500 + 40 + 6.

➪ The number is 546.
The number name is five hundred forty-six.

The expanded form is ____ + ____ + ____.

Guided Practice

I. **What number do the models show?**

Write the number, the number name, and the expanded form.

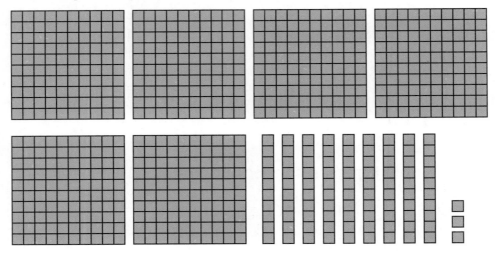

The models show ___6___ hundreds _____ tens _____ ones.

Write the 3-digit number that the models show. _____

The number name for the number that the models

show is _____.

Write the number in expanded form.

What is the value of the digit in the hundreds place? _____

What is the value of the digit in the tens place? _____

What is the value of the digit in the ones place? _____

The number in expanded form is _____.

2. **Write the number, the number name, and the expanded form to show 7 hundreds 0 tens 9 ones.**

Step 1

Write the number in a place-value chart.

hundreds	tens	ones
7		

Write the 3-digit number. _____

Write the number name. _____

Step 2

Write the number in expanded form.

What does the 7 in 709 stand for? _____ or _____

What does the 0 in 709 stand for? _____ or _____

What does the 9 in 709 stand for? _____ or _____

You do not write an addend for 0 in expanded form.

The number in expanded form is _____ + _____.

✺ Think•Pair•Share

MP3 3. Frank wrote the number name and the expanded form for 350 this way.

> Number name: three hundred fifty
> Expanded form: 300 + 5

Is Frank's work correct? Why or why not?

Independent Practice

Write the number that each model shows.

1.

_____ hundreds   _____ tens   _____ ones   _____

2.

_____ hundreds   _____ tens   _____ ones   _____

3.

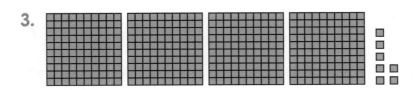

_____ hundreds   _____ tens   _____ ones   _____

4.

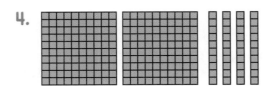

_____ hundreds   _____ tens   _____ ones   _____

Independent Practice

Match the number with its number name.

5. 915   six hundred eight

6. 730   eight hundred sixty

7. 443   nine hundred fifteen

8. 608   two hundred five

9. 860   seven hundred thirty

10. 205   four hundred forty-three

Write each number in expanded form.

11. 274 _____

12. 337 _____

13. 999 _____

14. 840 _____

15. 206 _____

16. 707 _____

Independent Practice

Circle the correct answer.

17. Which is the same as 700 + 40 + 3?   743   7,043   703

18. Which is the same as 400 + 50?   405   450   415

19. Which is the same as 200 + 40 + 5?   205   245   254

20. Which is the same as 800 + 8?   880   800   808

Write the number and the expanded form for each number name.

21. five hundred two   _____   _____

22. nine hundred ten   _____   _____

23. six hundred thirty-seven   _____   _____

24. one hundred eighty   _____   _____

Independent Practice

Circle the two ways that show the same number.

25. 340   three hundred forty-four $300 + 40 + 4$

26. 529   five hundred twenty-nine $500 + 2 + 9$

27. 902   nine hundred two $900 + 20$

28. 405   four hundred fifty $400 + 5$

MP3 **29.** Trevor wrote the number for three hundred ninety-seven in this place-value chart. Is his work correct? Why or why not?

hundreds	tens	ones
9	3	7

MP2 **30.** How many addends are in the expanded form of seven hundred three? How many digits are in that number? Do the number of addends and the number of digits match? Explain.

Essential Question:
How can you compare two numbers using the symbols >, <, = ?

Words to Know
greater than (>)
less than (<)
equal to (=)

Guided Instruction

In this lesson you will learn to compare two 3-digit numbers using place value.

Understand: Using place-value models to compare two numbers

Which number is greater, 152 or 125?

Place-value models can help you compare the numbers.

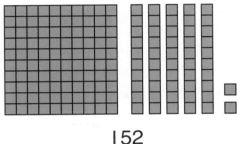

152

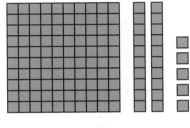

125

Start with the greatest place: hundreds

Compare the hundreds.
  Both 152 and 125 have 1 hundred.

Move on to the next greatest place: tens

Compare the tens.
  The number 152 has 5 tens.
  The number 125 has 2 tens.

So 152 is greater than 125, because 5 tens is greater than 2 tens.

Remember!
> means greater than.

▷ The number 152 is greater than the number 125.
  Write this as 152 > 125.

Guided Instruction

Understand: Using place-value charts to compare two numbers

Lucy has 382 stickers. Brady has 387 stickers. Who has fewer stickers?

Write both numbers in place-value charts.

hundreds	tens	ones
3	8	2

hundreds	tens	ones
3	8	7

Start with the greatest place: hundreds. Compare.
   382 and 387 both have 3 hundreds.

Move on to the next greatest place: tens. Compare.
   382 and 387 both have 8 tens.

Move on to the last place: ones. Compare.
   382 has 2 ones. 387 has 7 ones.

So 382 is less than 387 because 2 is less than 7.
   382 < 387

Remember!
< means less than.

▷ Lucy has fewer stickers than Brady.

Understand: Comparing numbers with the same digits in the same places

Which number is greater, 187 or 187?

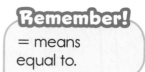
Remember!
= means equal to.

Compare hundreds, tens, and ones.
The hundreds, tens, and ones are the same.

▷ So 187 is equal to 187. Write 187 = 187.

Guided Instruction

Connect: Use place value and symbols to compare two 3-digit numbers

Compare 684 and 677. Use >, <, or = in your answer.

Step 1

Use place value to compare 684 and 677.

684 = ___6___ hundreds ___8___ tens ___4___ ones

677 = ___6___ hundreds ___7___ tens ___7___ ones

Start with the greatest place-value position.

Which place will you look at first? ___hundreds___

Compare. 684 and 677 both have ___6___ hundreds.

Step 2

Compare the digits in the next greatest place.

684 has ___8___ tens. 677 has ___7___ tens.

8 tens is greater than 7 tens.

684 is greater than 677.

Step 3

Write the symbol <, >, or = to compare. 684 (>) 677

▷ 684 > 677

Write *true* or *false*.

406 > 416 _____   509 < 499 _____   746 = 746 _____

Guided Practice

I. **Write >, <, or = to compare: 989 ● 998**

Step 1

989 = ____ hundreds ____ tens ____ ones

998 = ____ hundreds ____ tens ____ ones

First compare the _____.

989 and 998 both have ____ hundreds.

Step 2

Next compare the _____.

989 has ____ tens. 998 has ____ tens.

8 is _____ than 9. So 989 is _____ than 998.

Step 3

Write >, <, or =.

989 ◯ 998

⁔⁎ Think•Pair•Share

MP2 2. Compare. Write > or <.

998 ◯ 989   989 ◯ 998

Tell how your comparisons are alike and how they are different.

Independent Practice

**Write the numbers that the models show.
Compare. Circle the greater number.**

1.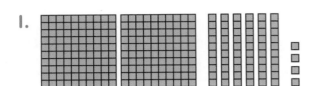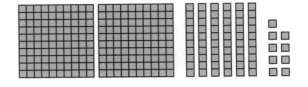

   _____   _____

2.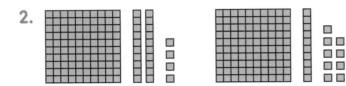

   _____   _____

**Write numbers that the models show.
Compare. Circle the lesser number.**

3.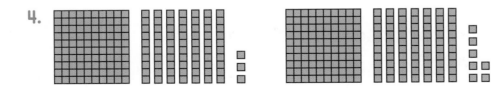

   _____   _____

4.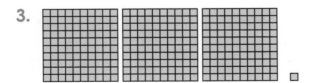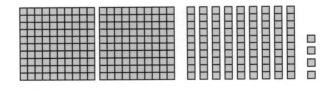

   _____   _____

Independent Practice

Compare. Write *greater than*, *less than*, or *equal to*.

5.

hundreds	tens	ones
7	3	7

hundreds	tens	ones
7	7	3

737 is _____ 773.

6.

hundreds	tens	ones
4	8	5

hundreds	tens	ones
4	8	1

485 is _____ 481.

7.

hundreds	tens	ones
9	2	7

hundreds	tens	ones
9	2	9

927 is _____ 929.

8.

hundreds	tens	ones
7	9	6

hundreds	tens	ones
7	5	9

796 is _____ 759.

Independent Practice

Compare. Circle your answer.

9. 842 is ____ 842.   greater than   less than   (equal to)

10. 399 is ____ 404.   greater than   (less than)   equal to

11. 205 is ____ 215.   greater than   (less than)   equal to

Compare. Write >, <, or =.

12. 457 (<) 475

13. 730 (>) 729

14. 837 (>) 799

15. 381 (=) 381

16. 199 (<) 201

17. 535 (<) 539

18. 288 (<) 298

19. 639 (>) 637

20. 949 (=) 949

21. 102 (<) 121

22. 715 (>) 713

23. 559 (<) 619

24. 348 (>) 347

25. 190 (>) 189

Independent Practice

MP3 **26.** When you are comparing two 3-digit numbers, why do you think it is important to look first at the digits that have the greatest values?

MP3 **27.** Amy collects 388 bottles for recycling. Brian collects 391 bottles for recycling. Who collects more bottles? Explain how you know. Use place value.

MP6 **28.** Frannie has 156 buttons in a jar. Louise has a jar with fewer buttons than Frannie has. Which could be Louise's jar of buttons? Explain your answer.

158 buttons

154 buttons

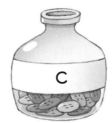
161 buttons

10 Add Two-Digit Numbers

Essential Question:
How can you add two 2-digit numbers?

Words to Know
regroup

Guided Instruction

In this lesson you will learn different ways to add within 100 using place value.

Understand: Using place value to add two 2-digit numbers

Mike has 16 toy cars.
Oscar has 23 toy cars.
How many toy cars do they have in all?

Write an addition equation.

16 + 23 = ▪

Use models for the tens and ones.

16 = 1 ten 6 ones   23 = 2 tens 3 ones

16   +   23

Add the ones.

6 ones + 3 ones = 9 ones

3 tens 9 ones = 39

So 16 + 23 = 39.

Add the tens.

1 ten + 2 tens = 3 tens

▷ Mike and Oscar have 39 toy cars in all.

Understand: Using properties to add two 2-digit numbers

There are 59 coins in a jar.
Riley adds 33 more.
How many coins are in the jar now?

Write an addition equation.

$59 + 33 = $ ▨

Break up each addend into tens and ones.

$50 + 9 + 30 + 3 = $ ▨

Change the order of the 9 and the 30 to put the tens together and the ones together.

Remember!
Changing the order of the addends does not change the sum.

$50 + 30 + 9 + 3$

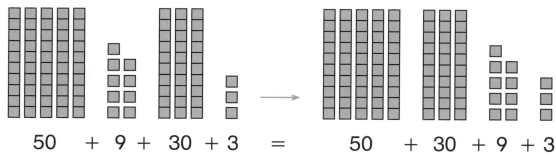

$50 \quad + 9 + 30 + 3 \quad = \quad 50 \quad + 30 + 9 + 3$

Add the ones.

$9 + 3 = 12$

$80 + 12 = 92$

So $59 + 33 = $ __92__.

Add the tens.

$50 + 30 = 80$

⇨ There are 92 coins in the jar.

Guided Instruction

Connect: Add two 2-digit numbers regrouping ones

Add: 45 + 29 = ■

Step 1

Write the addition in a place-value chart.

tens	ones
4	5
+ 2	9

Step 2

Add the ones.

5 ones + 9 ones = ____ ones

You can regroup 14 ones as one ten and some ones.

14 ones = ____ ten ____ ones

You can show regrouping 14 ones in the place-value chart.

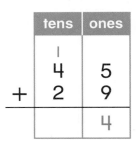

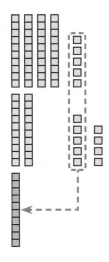

Step 3

Add the tens.

4 tens + 2 tens + 1 ten = ____ tens

▷ 45 + 29 = ____

tens	ones
1	
4	5
+ 2	9
7	4

Remember!
Add the ten you made to the other tens.

I. **Add: 24 + 58 =** ▇

Step 1

Write the addition
in a place-value chart.

tens	ones
2	4
+ 5	8

Step 2

Add the ones.

4 ones + 8 ones = ___12___ ones

You can make a ten.

12 ones = ___ ten ___ ones

Use the place-value chart to show
how you regroup the ones.

tens	ones
1	
2	4
+ 5	8
	2

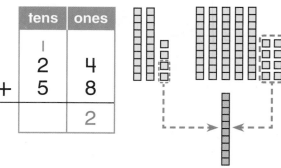

Step 3

Add the tens.

2 tens + 5 tens + 1 ten = ___ tens

24 + 58 = ___

tens	ones
1	
2	4
+ 5	8
	2

Think•Pair•Share

MP2 **2.** Frank has 19 baseball cards. Wally has 31.
How many baseball cards do they have in all?
Explain how you regroup to find your answer.

Independent Practice

1. Add. $13 + 34 =$ ◼

Add the ones.

3 ones + 4 ones = ____ ones

Can you make a ten? ____

Add the tens.

1 ten + 3 tens = ____ tens

$13 + 34 =$ ____

tens	ones
1	3
+ 3	4

2. $47 + 25 =$ ◼

Add the ones.

7 ones + 5 ones = ____ ones

Can you make a ten? ____

12 ones = ____ ten ____ ones

Add the tens.

4 tens + 2 tens + 1 ten = ____ tens

$47 + 25 =$ ____

tens	ones
4	7
+ 2	5

Add.

3.

tens	ones
2	2
+ 5	1

4.

tens	ones
6	7
+ 2	4

5.

tens	ones
3	9
+ 1	4

6.

tens	ones
4	8
+ 2	6

7.

tens	ones
3	5
+ 1	6

8.

tens	ones
3	6
+ 5	1

9.

tens	ones
4	2
+ 4	7

10.

tens	ones
5	6
+ 3	6

Independent Practice

Circle the correct answer.

11. $32 + 18 = \blacksquare$ 40   50   410

12. $24 + 22 = \blacksquare$ 46   56   66

13. $59 + 19 = \blacksquare$ 68   78   69

Add.

14.
```
  1 7
+ 4 8
```

15.
```
  5 4
+ 2 9
```

16.
```
  6 6
+ 2 3
```

17.
```
  2 9
+ 2 9
```

18.
```
  1 4
+ 3 8
```

19.
```
  1 3
+ 4 7
```

20.
```
  3 4
+ 2 5
```

21.
```
  1 6
+ 5 8
```

22.
```
  1 6
+ 3 4
```

MP2 **23.** Emily has 69 beads. Sarah has 27. How many beads do they have in all? Write an equation for the problem. Solve the problem in two ways. Talk about each way.

One way: Break addends into tens and ones.

Another way: Use regrouping.

Subtract Two-Digit Numbers

Essential Question:
How can you subtract a 2-digit number from a 2-digit number?

Guided Instruction

In this lesson you will learn how to subtract 2-digit numbers.

Understand: Subtracting 2-digit numbers using place-value models

> There are 57 stickers on a sheet.
> Marcus uses 34 of the stickers.
> How many stickers are left?

Write a subtraction equation.

57 − 34 = ▨

Use models.
Cross out as you subtract.

57 = 5 tens 7 ones   34 = 3 tens 4 ones

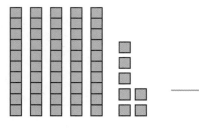   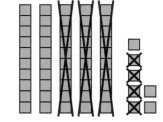

First subtract the ones.
   7 ones − 4 ones = 3 ones

Then subtract the tens.
   5 tens − 3 tens = 2 tens

5 tens 7 ones − 3 tens 4 ones = 2 tens 3 ones
   57 − 34 = 23

▷ There are 23 stickers left.

Understand: Subtracting 2-digit numbers using place-value charts

Lori has 38 marbles.
She gives 23 marbles to a friend.
How many marbles does Lori have now?

Write a subtraction equation.

38 − 23 = ▨

Step 1

Write the subtraction in a
place-value chart.

Step 2

Subtract the ones.

8 ones − 3 ones = 5 ones

tens	ones
3	8
2	3
	5

Step 3

Subtract the tens.

3 tens − 2 tens = 1 ten

38 − 23 = __15__

tens	ones
3	8
2	3
1	5

▷ Lori has _____ marbles now.

Guided Instruction

Connect: Subtracting 2-digit numbers with regrouping 1 ten as 10 ones

Subtract: 64 − 39 = ■

Step 1

Write the subtraction in a place-value chart.

Step 2

To subtract 9 ones from 6 tens 4 ones, first regroup 1 ten as 10 ones. 5 tens are left.

Add the 10 ones to the 4 ones. 4 ones + 10 ones = 14 ones.

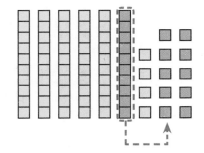

tens	ones
5 6̸	14 4̸
− 3	9

Step 3

Subtract ones.

14 ones − 9 ones = __5__ ones

tens	ones
5 6̸	14 4̸
− 3	9
	5

Step 4

Subtract tens.

5 tens − 3 tens = __2__ tens

➡ 64 − 39 = __25__

tens	ones
5 6̸	14 4̸
− 3	9
2	5

1. **Subtract: 82 − 47 =** ▩

Step 1

Write the subtraction in a
place-value chart.

tens	ones
8	2
− 4	7

Step 2

To subtract 7 ones from 8 tens 2 ones,

first regroup 1 ten as __10__ ones.

Add the 10 ones to the 2 ones.
Subtract the 1 ten from the 8 tens.

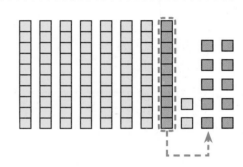

Step 3

Use the place-value chart to show that 82 = 7 tens _____ ones.

Subtract the ones.

_____ ones − _____ ones = _____ ones

Subtract the tens.

_____ tens − _____ tens = _____ tens

82 − 47 = _____

tens	ones
7	12
8̸	2̸
− 4	7

★♥★ Think•Pair•Share

MP7 2. Do you need to regroup to subtract 36 from 61?
Without subtracting, explain why or why not.

Independent Practice

Subtract.

1. $67 - 46 = \blacksquare$

   Subtract the ones.

tens	ones
6	7
− 4	6

   ____ ones − ____ ones = ____ one

   Subtract the tens.

   ____ tens − ____ tens = ____ tens

   $67 - 46 =$ ____

2. $83 - 39 = \blacksquare$

   Can you subtract 9 ones from 3 ones?

tens	ones
8	3
− 3	9

   _____

   Regroup 1 ten as 10 ones.

   Add 10 ones to the 3 ones.

   Subtract 1 ten from the 8 tens.

   8 tens 3 ones = ____ tens ____ ones

   Subtract the ones.

   _____ ones − ____ ones = ____ ones

   Subtract the tens.

   ____ tens − ____ tens = ____ tens

   $83 - 39 =$ ____

Independent Practice

3.

tens	ones
4	9
− 3	6

4.

tens	ones
6	5
− 2	4

5.

tens	ones
6	3
− 2	8

6.

tens	ones
3	5
− 2	4

7.

tens	ones
5	0
− 2	9

8.

tens	ones
7	6
− 3	9

9.

tens	ones
5	3
− 3	8

10.

tens	ones
8	3
− 2	2

Independent Practice

Circle the correct answer.

11. $79 - 34 = $ ▣   35   45   113

12. $51 - 16 = $ ▣   67   35   45

13. $64 - 56 = $ ▣   18   120   8

Subtract.

14.
$$\begin{array}{r} 59 \\ -18 \\ \hline \end{array}$$

15.
$$\begin{array}{r} 67 \\ -29 \\ \hline \end{array}$$

16.
$$\begin{array}{r} 97 \\ -45 \\ \hline \end{array}$$

17.
$$\begin{array}{r} 41 \\ -23 \\ \hline \end{array}$$

18.
$$\begin{array}{r} 86 \\ -32 \\ \hline \end{array}$$

19.
$$\begin{array}{r} 65 \\ -38 \\ \hline \end{array}$$

20.
$$\begin{array}{r} 94 \\ -35 \\ \hline \end{array}$$

21.
$$\begin{array}{r} 73 \\ -45 \\ \hline \end{array}$$

22.
$$\begin{array}{r} 82 \\ -48 \\ \hline \end{array}$$

MP2 **23.** Without subtracting, tell which subtraction equation will have the greater answer.

$$74 - 68 = \blacksquare \quad \text{or} \quad 83 - 68 = \blacksquare$$

Talk about your answer.

MP3 **24.** Marco says that he can use addition to check that his subtraction is correct. Marco's work is shown below. Finish what Marco started.

$$
\begin{array}{r}
{}^{5}^{12} \\
\cancel{6}\,2 \\
-\,2\,7 \\
\hline
3\,5
\end{array}
\qquad
\begin{array}{r}
{}^{1} \\
3\,5 \\
+ \\
\hline
\end{array}
$$

Is Marco's subtraction correct? Why can you use addition to check subtraction?

12 Add More Than Two Numbers

Guided Instruction

In this lesson you will learn how to add up to four 2-digit numbers.

Understand: You can add three 2-digit numbers using place value

Tia has 32 pennies.
Leo has 23 pennies.
Albert has 24 pennies.
How many pennies do they have in all?

Write an addition equation.
$32 + 23 + 24 = $ ▪

Use models to show the tens and ones in each addend.

$32 = 30 + 2$

$23 = 20 + 3$

$24 = 20 + 4$

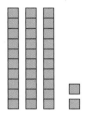 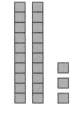 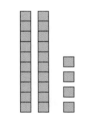

$30 + 2$ $20 + 3$ $20 + 4$

Add the ones.
$2 + 3 = 5$ and $5 + 4 = 9$

Add the tens.
$30 + 20 = 50$ and $50 + 20 = 70$

Put the tens and ones together: $70 + 9 = 79$
$32 + 23 + 24 = 79$

▷ They have 79 pennies in all.

Guided Instruction

Understand: Grouping addends to add three 2-digit numbers

There are 25 red marbles, 42 green marbles, and 15 blue marbles in a bag.
How many marbles in all are in the bag?

Write an addition equation.

$25 + 42 + 15 = \blacksquare$

Break each addend into tens and ones.

$25 = 20 + 5 \qquad 42 = 40 + 2 \qquad 15 = 10 + 5$

Add the ones.

$5 + 2 + 5 = \blacksquare$

You can change the order of the addends and make 10.

Remember!
Changing the order of the addends does not change the sum.
$5 + 2 + 5 = 5 + 5 + 2$

$5 + 2 + 5$

$\qquad 5 + 5 = 10$

$\qquad 10 + 2 = 12$

$12 = 1$ ten 2 ones

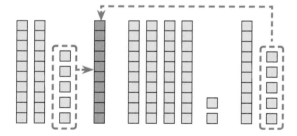

Add the tens.

Remember!
Add the new ten.

$20 + 40 + 10 + 10 = \underline{80}$

Put the tens and ones together: $80 + 2 = \underline{82}$

$25 + 42 + 15 = \underline{\hspace{1cm}}$

➢ There are _____ marbles in the bag.

Guided Instruction

Connect: Connect adding three 2-digit numbers to adding four 2-digit numbers

Add: 21 + 23 + 19 + 26 = ▪

Step 1

Write the addition in a place-value chart.

Step 2

tens	ones
1	
2	1
2	3
1	9
+ 2	6
	9

Add the ones.

1 one + 3 ones = 4 ones

4 ones + 9 ones = 13 ones

13 ones + 6 ones = 19 ones

Make a new ten: 19 = 1 ten 9 ones

tens	ones
1	
2	1
2	3
1	9
+ 2	6
8	9

Add the tens.

2 tens + 2 tens = 4 tens

4 tens + 1 ten = 5 tens

5 tens + 2 tens = 7 tens

7 tens + 1 ten = 8 tens

Remember!

Add the ten you made to the other tens.

8 tens 9 ones = ___89___

▷ 21 + 23 + 19 + 26 = _____

1. **Add: 12 + 36 + 25 + 14 = ▨**

Step 1

Write the addition in a place-value chart.

tens	ones
1	2
3	6
2	5
+ 1	4

Add the ones.

2 ones + 6 ones = _____ ones

8 ones + 5 ones = _____ ones

13 ones + 4 ones = _____ ones

17 ones = _____ ten _____ ones

Step 2

tens	ones
1	2
3	6
2	5
+ 1	4

Add the tens you see in the place-value chart.

1 ten + 3 tens = _____ tens

4 tens + 2 tens = _____ tens

6 tens + 1 ten = _____ tens

Add the new ten:

7 tens + 1 ten = _____ tens

8 tens 7 ones = _____

12 + 36 + 25 + 14 = _____

 **Think•Pair•Share**

MP7 2. Four 2-digit numbers have a sum of 86. Three of the numbers are 24, 28, and 15. What is the fourth number? Talk about how you know.

Independent Practice

Add.

1. $42 + 25 + 22 = \blacksquare$

   $2 + 5 + \underline{\quad} = \underline{\quad}$

   $40 + 20 + \underline{\quad} = \underline{\quad}$

   $42 + 25 + 22 = \underline{\quad}$

tens	ones
4	2
2	5
+ 2	2

2. $24 + 36 + 21 + 16 = \blacksquare$

   $4 + 6 + \underline{\quad} + \underline{\quad} = \underline{\quad}$

   $17 = 1 \text{ ten } \underline{\quad} \text{ ones}$

   $20 + \underline{\quad} + 20 + \underline{\quad} + \underline{\quad} = \underline{\quad}$

   $24 + 36 + 21 + 16 = \underline{\quad}$

tens	ones
2	4
3	6
2	1
+ 1	6

3. $32 + 16 + 34 + 11 = \blacksquare$

   $2 + 6 + \underline{\quad} + \underline{\quad} = \underline{\quad}$

   $13 = 1 \text{ ten } \underline{\quad} \text{ ones}$

   $30 + \underline{\quad} + 30 + \underline{\quad} + \underline{\quad} = \underline{\quad}$

   $32 + 16 + 34 + 11 = \underline{\quad}$

tens	ones
3	2
1	6
3	4
+ 1	1

Independent Practice

Add.

4. $29 + 31 + 24 =$ ■

tens	ones
2 3 2	9 1 4

$+$

$29 + 31 + 24 =$ ____

5. $26 + 25 + 14 =$ ■

tens	ones
2 2 1	6 5 4

$+$

$26 + 25 + 14 =$ ____

6. $53 + 12 + 28 =$ ■

tens	ones
5 1 2	3 2 8

$+$

$53 + 12 + 28 =$ ____

7. $35 + 21 + 15 =$ ■

tens	ones
3 2 1	5 1 5

$+$

$35 + 21 + 15 =$ ____

8. $12 + 37 + 16 + 22 =$ ■

tens	ones
1 3 1 2	2 7 6 2

$+$

$12 + 37 + 16 + 22 =$ ____

9. $25 + 23 + 15 + 26 =$ ■

tens	ones
2 2 1 2	5 3 5 6

$+$

$25 + 23 + 15 + 26 =$ ____

Independent Practice

Circle the correct answer.

10. $51 + 10 + 19 = $ ▨   70   80   89

11. $43 + 17 + 29 = $ ▨   89   79   70

12. $23 + 31 + 16 = $ ▨   60   70   80

13. $20 + 18 + 24 = $ ▨   52   60   62

Add.

14.
```
  41
  28
+ 17
```

15.
```
  32
  13
+ 27
```

16.
```
  41
  17
+ 24
```

17.
```
  34
  16
+ 29
```

18.
```
  36
  17
  23
+ 12
```

19.
```
  27
  15
  14
+ 33
```

20.
```
  31
  24
  19
+ 25
```

21.
```
  11
  28
  22
+ 35
```

MP1 **22.** A jar has 90 buttons in it. There are 21 red buttons, 19 yellow buttons, and 36 green buttons. The rest of the buttons are blue. How many blue buttons are there? Talk about how you found your answer.

MP3 **23.** Rod added 38 + 13 + 22. His answer was 63. Was his answer correct? If not, talk about what mistake he made.

MP1 **24.** Make up a word problem for which you need to add three or four 2-digit numbers to solve. Write and solve an equation for your word problem.

Add Three-Digit Numbers within 1,000

Guided Instruction

In this lesson you will learn how to add three-digit numbers.

Understand: Adding 3-digit numbers without regrouping

Add: $134 + 125 = \blacksquare$

Use models and a place-value chart.

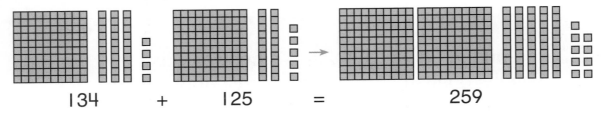

134 + 125 = 259

Add the ones: $4 + 5 = 9$
Add the tens: $30 + 20 = 50$
Add the hundreds: $100 + 100 = 200$

	hundreds	tens	ones
	1	3	4
+	1	2	5
	2	5	9

▷ $134 + 125 = 259$

Understand: Adding 3-digit numbers by regrouping ones

Add: $156 + 239 = \blacksquare$

Add the ones: $6 + 9 = 15$
Make 1 ten from 10 ones: $15 = 1$ ten 5 ones
Add the tens: $50 + 30 + 10 = 90$
Add the hundreds: $100 + 200 = 300$

	hundreds	tens	ones
		1	
	1	5	6
+	2	3	9
	3	9	5

▷ $156 + 239 = 395$

Understand: Adding two 3-digit numbers with regrouping tens to make a hundred

Lisa has 183 seashells.
Kendra has 142 seashells.
How many seashells do they have in all?

Write an equation.

183 + 142 = ▨

Use models and a place-value chart to show the addition.

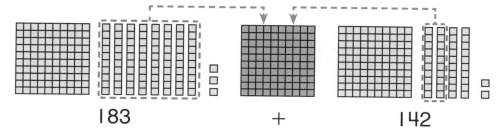

183   +   142

Add the ones.

    3 ones + 2 ones = 5 ones

3 + 2 = 5

Add the tens.

    8 tens + 4 tens = 12 tens

You can make 1 hundred from 10 tens.

12 tens = ___ hundred ___ tens

hundreds	tens	ones
1		
1	8	3
+ 1	4	2
3	2	5

Remember!
Add the hundred that you made from 10 tens.

Add the hundreds.

    1 hundred + 1 hundred + 1 hundred = 3 hundreds

100 + 100 + 100 = 300

183 + 142 = 325

▷ Lisa and Kendra have _____ seashells in all.

Guided Instruction

Connect: Addition with regrouping both tens and ones

Blake read 186 pages of one book and 175 pages of another book. How many pages was that altogether?

186 + 175 = ▪

Step 1

Write the addition in a place-value chart.

Step 2

Add the ones.
6 ones + 5 ones = 11 ones

Make a ten:
11 ones = 1 ten 1 one

hundreds	tens	ones
	1	
1	8	6
+ 1	7	5
		1

Step 3

Add the tens.

8 tens + 7 tens + 1 ten = __16__ tens

Make a hundred:

16 tens = ____ hundred ____ tens

hundreds	tens	ones
	1	
1	8	6
+ 1	7	5
	6	1

Step 4

Add the hundreds.

100 + 100 + 100 = _____

186 + 175 = __361__

hundreds	tens	ones
	1	
1	8	6
+ 1	7	5
3	6	1

▷ Blake read _____ pages altogether.

1. **Add: 248 + 155 = ▨**

Step 1

Add the ones.

8 ones + 5 ones = ___ ones

You can make a ten.

13 ones = ___ ten ___ ones

hundreds	tens	ones
2	4	8
+ 1	5	5
		3

Step 2

Add the tens.

Remember to add the ten you made.

4 tens + 5 tens + 1 ten = ___ tens
You can make a hundred.

10 tens = ___ hundred ___ tens

hundreds	tens	ones
2	4	8
+ 1	5	5
	0	3

Step 3

Add the hundreds.

Remember to add the hundred you made.

2 hundreds + 1 hundred + 1 hundred = ___ hundreds

248 + 155 = _____

Think•Pair•Share

MP2 2. Without adding, tell which sum is greater, 479 + 35 or 479 + 350. Talk about how you know.

Independent Practice

Add. Show your work on the place-value chart.

1. $136 + 72 = $ ■

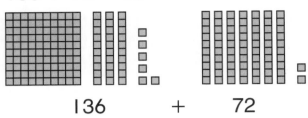

136   +   72

Add the ones.
Can you make a ten? _____

Add the tens.
Can you make a hundred? _____

Add the hundreds.

$136 + 72 = $ _____

hundreds	tens	ones
1	3	6
+	7	2

2. $159 + 152 = $ ■

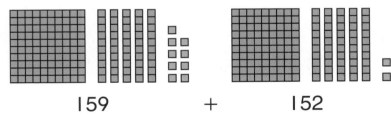

159   +   152

Add the ones.
Can you make a ten? _____

Add the tens.
Can you make
a hundred? _____

Add the hundreds.

$159 + 152 = $ _____

hundreds	tens	ones
1	5	9
+ 1	5	2

Independent Practice

Add.

3.

hundreds	tens	ones
1	4	2
+ 2	3	6

4.

hundreds	tens	ones
1	1	5
+ 3	2	7

5.

hundreds	tens	ones
4	7	3
+	3	4

6.

hundreds	tens	ones
1	4	6
+ 4	9	2

7.

hundreds	tens	ones
4	8	9
+ 2	0	5

8.

hundreds	tens	ones
2	7	8
+ 3	4	1

9.

hundreds	tens	ones
2	4	2
+ 6	9	9

10.

hundreds	tens	ones
7	5	6
+ 1	4	6

Independent Practice

Circle the correct answer.

11. 302 + 181 = ■　　　383　　　483　　　493

12. 245 + 229 = ■　　　474　　　464　　　574

13. 159 + 222 = ■　　　391　　　381　　　371

Add.

14. $\begin{array}{r} 438 \\ +381 \\ \hline \end{array}$

15. $\begin{array}{r} 342 \\ +227 \\ \hline \end{array}$

16. $\begin{array}{r} 283 \\ +241 \\ \hline \end{array}$

17. $\begin{array}{r} 178 \\ +443 \\ \hline \end{array}$

18. $\begin{array}{r} 156 \\ +336 \\ \hline \end{array}$

19. $\begin{array}{r} 552 \\ +267 \\ \hline \end{array}$

20. $\begin{array}{r} 504 \\ +268 \\ \hline \end{array}$

21. $\begin{array}{r} 197 \\ +336 \\ \hline \end{array}$

22. $\begin{array}{r} 604 \\ +198 \\ \hline \end{array}$

Independent Practice

Solve each problem.

23. Mr. Kent drives 214 miles on Monday. On Tuesday, he drives 258 miles. How many miles does Mr. Kent drive in all?

    Mr. Kent drives ____ miles in all.

24. Alex has 345 soccer cards and 365 baseball cards. How many cards does he have altogether?

    Alex has ____ cards altogether.

MP1 25. There are three grades at the Clark School. There are 268 children in the first grade. There are 324 children in the second grade. There are 297 children in the third grade. How many children go to the Clark School? Talk about how to solve the problem.

MP3 26. Bradley added 163 + 428. His work is shown below.

$$\begin{array}{r} 163 \\ +428 \\ \hline 581 \end{array}$$

What did Bradley do wrong? Show the correct way to solve the problem.

Subtract Three-Digit Numbers within 1,000

Essential Question: How can you subtract three-digit numbers?

Guided Instruction

In this lesson you will learn how to subtract three-digit numbers.

Understand: Subtracting two 3-digit numbers without regrouping

Subtract: $287 - 135 = \blacksquare$

Use a place-value chart.
Subtract the ones: $7 - 5 = 2$
Subtract the tens: $80 - 30 = 50$
Subtract the hundreds:
$\quad 200 - 100 = 100$

hundreds	tens	ones
2	8	7
− 1	3	5
1	5	2

▷ $287 - 135 = 152$

Understand: Subtracting two 3-digit numbers regrouping a ten

Subtract: $252 - 113 = \blacksquare$

Use a place-value chart.
You cannot subtract 3 ones from 2 ones.
Make 10 ones from 1 ten.
$\quad$ 1 ten 2 ones = 12 ones
Now 4 tens are left.
Subtract the ones: $12 - 3 = 9$
Subtract the tens: $40 - 10 = 30$
Subtract the hundreds: $200 - 100 = 100$

hundreds	tens	ones
2	$\overset{4}{\cancel{5}}$	$\overset{12}{\cancel{2}}$
− 1	1	3
1	3	9

▷ $252 - 113 = 139$

Guided Instruction

Understand: Subtracting two 3-digit numbers regrouping a hundred

Marcie read a book with 356 pages.
Shane read a book with 184 pages.
How many more pages did Marcie read than Shane?

Write an equation.

$356 - 184 = \blacksquare$

Use a place-value chart to show the subtraction.

hundreds	tens	ones
3	5	6
− 1	8	4

Subtract the ones: $6 - 4 = 2$

You cannot subtract 8 tens from 5 tens.
Make 10 tens from 1 hundred.
3 hundreds 5 tens = 2 hundreds 15 tens
Now you can subtract tens.

hundreds	tens	ones
2 3̶	15 5̶	6
− 1	8	4
		2

$15 \text{ tens} - 8 \text{ tens} = \underline{7} \text{ tens}$

Subtract the hundreds:
2 hundreds − 1 hundred = 1 hundred
$356 - 184 = 172$

hundreds	tens	ones
2 3̶	15 5̶	6
− 1	8	4
	7	2

▷ Marcie read 172 more pages than Shane.

Guided Instruction

Connect: Subtraction with regrouping both a ten and a hundred

> Emile has 320 pennies. He gives 195 to his sister. How many pennies does Emile have left?

Write an equation: $320 - 195 = \blacksquare$

Step 1

Write the subtraction in a place-value chart.
Make 10 ones from 1 ten.
Subtract the ones.

10 ones − 5 ones = _____ 5 ones

hundreds	tens	ones
3	1 $\not{2}$	10 $\not{0}$
− 1	9	5
		5

Step 2

Make 10 tens from 1 hundred.
Add the new tens to the 1 ten you had left after making 10 ones.

1 ten + 10 tens = _____ tens

Subtract the tens:

11 tens − 9 tens = _____ tens

hundreds	tens	ones
2 $\not{3}$	11 $\not{1}$ $\not{2}$	10 $\not{0}$
− 1	9	5
	2	5

Step 3

Subtract the hundreds:

2 hundreds − 1 hundred = _____ hundred

$320 - 195 =$ _____

➡ Emile has _____ pennies left.

hundreds	tens	ones
2 $\not{3}$	11 $\not{1}$ $\not{2}$	10 $\not{0}$
− 1	9	5
	2	5

Guided Practice

I. Subtract: 532 − 253 = ▢

Step 1

Are there enough ones to subtract? _____

Make _____ ones from 1 ten.

10 ones + 2 ones = _____ ones

_____ ones − 3 ones = _____ ones

hundreds	tens	ones
	2	12
5	̶3̶	̶2̶
− 2	5	3
		9

Step 2

How many tens are left? _____

Are there enough tens to subtract? _____

Make _____ tens from 1 hundred.

10 tens + 2 tens = _____ tens

_____ tens − 5 tens = _____ tens

hundreds	tens	ones
	12	
4	̶2̶	12
̶5̶	̶3̶	̶2̶
− 2	5	3
	7	9

Step 3

How many hundreds are left? _____
Subtract the hundreds.

400 − 200 = _____

532 − 253 = _____

hundreds	tens	ones
	12	
4	̶2̶	12
̶5̶	̶3̶	̶2̶
− 2	5	3
	7	9

 Think•Pair•Share

MP7 **2.** Talk about how you can tell without subtracting if you need to make more tens or ones.

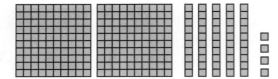

Independent Practice

Subtract.

1. 254 − 137 = ▨

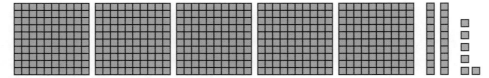

hundreds	tens	ones
2	5	4
− 1	3	7

Are there enough ones

to subtract 7 ones? _____

Regroup 1 ten as 10 ones.

  4 ones + 10 ones = _____ ones

Subtract the ones, tens, and hundreds.

  254 − 137 = _____

---

2. 526 − 274 = ▨

Subtract the ones.

Are there enough tens

to subtract 7 tens? _____

hundreds	tens	ones
5	2	6
− 2	7	4

Regroup 1 hundred as 10 tens.

  2 tens + 10 tens = _____ tens

Subtract the tens and hundreds.

  526 − 274 = _____

Independent Practice

Subtract.

3.
hundreds	tens	ones
7	5	8
− 2	3	1

4.
hundreds	tens	ones
4	6	3
− 1	2	7

5.
hundreds	tens	ones
1	7	3
−	2	4

6.
hundreds	tens	ones
6	4	5
− 4	9	2

7.
hundreds	tens	ones
4	0	9
− 2	5	7

8.
hundreds	tens	ones
2	3	9
− 1	5	6

9.
hundreds	tens	ones
8	4	6
− 3	8	7

10.
hundreds	tens	ones
7	6	2
− 1	7	6

Independent Practice

Circle the correct answer.

11. $239 - 129 = $ ▧   100   110   210

12. $345 - 182 = $ ▧   163   243   263

Subtract.

13.
$$\begin{array}{r} 634 \\ -519 \\ \hline \end{array}$$

14.
$$\begin{array}{r} 388 \\ -263 \\ \hline \end{array}$$

15.
$$\begin{array}{r} 582 \\ -265 \\ \hline \end{array}$$

16.
$$\begin{array}{r} 724 \\ -445 \\ \hline \end{array}$$

17.
$$\begin{array}{r} 628 \\ -283 \\ \hline \end{array}$$

18.
$$\begin{array}{r} 427 \\ -289 \\ \hline \end{array}$$

Solve each problem.

19. Zach is flying 723 miles on an airplane. The plane makes a stop after going 472 miles. How far is the rest of the flight?

The rest of the flight is

_____ miles.

20. Isabelle has 856 stamps in her stamp collection. Akeem has 512 stamps in his collection. How many more stamps does Isabelle have?

Isabelle has _____ more stamps.

Independent Practice

MP3 **21.** Drew started with a 3-digit number and made 10 tens from 1 hundred. He then had 8 hundreds 14 tens 7 ones. Megan said that Drew must have started with the number 747. Is Megan correct? Talk about why or why not.

MP2 **22.** Show what you know about regrouping. Write and solve a problem for subtracting a 3-digit number from 653 by regrouping 1 hundred as 10 tens. Talk about why the number you chose involves regrouping 1 hundred as 10 tens.

MP7 **23.** List all the 3-digit numbers that can be subtracted from 210 that do not involve any regrouping. Talk about how you know that these numbers do not need to be regrouped.

Essential Question:
How can you use mental math to add or subtract 10 or 100?

Guided Instruction

In this lesson you will learn how to use mental math to add or subtract 10 or 100.

Understand: When you add or subtract 10, the digit in the tens place changes

Jamie read 236 pages last month.
Evan read 10 more pages than Jamie.
How many pages did Evan read?
Marta read 10 fewer pages than Jamie.
How many pages did Marta read?

Remember!
You can add to find more.

You can subtract to find fewer or less.

Find the number of pages Evan read.

Add: $236 + 10 = $ ▮

When you add 10, the digit in the tens place changes. In 236, the 3 that shows **30** changes to a 4 that shows **40**.
$236 + 10 = 246$

hundreds	tens	ones
2	**3**	6

↓ **30 + 10 = 40**

hundreds	tens	ones
2	**4**	6

Find the number of pages Marta read.

Subtract: $236 - 10 = $ ▮

When you subtract 10, the digit in the tens place changes. In 236, the 3 that shows **30** changes to a 2 that shows **20**.
$236 - 10 = 226$

hundreds	tens	ones
2	**3**	6

↓ **30 - 10 = 20**

hundreds	tens	ones
2	**2**	6

▷ Evan read 246 pages. Marta read 226 pages.

Understand: When you add or subtract 100, the digit in the hundreds place changes

> Clark has 348 trading cards.
> Jesse has 100 more trading cards than Clark.
> How many trading cards does Jesse have?
> Saher has 100 fewer trading cards than Clark.
> How many trading cards does Saher have?

Find the number of trading cards Jesse has.

Add: $348 + 100 =$ ▨

When you add 100, the digit in the hundreds place changes. In 348, the 3 that shows **300** changes to a 4 that shows **400**.

$348 + 100 = 448$

hundreds	tens	ones
3	4	8

$300 + 100 = 400$

hundreds	tens	ones
4	4	8

Find the number of trading cards Saher has.

Subtract: $348 - 100 =$ ▨

When you subtract 100, the digit in the hundreds place changes. In 348, the 3 that shows **300** changes to a 2 that shows **200**.

$348 - 100 = 248$

hundreds	tens	ones
3	4	8

$300 - 100 = 200$

hundreds	tens	ones
2	4	8

▷ Jesse has 448 trading cards.
   Saher has 248 trading cards.

Guided Instruction

Connect: What you know about adding and subtracting 10 or 100

La Vae wrote these two number patterns.
Pattern A: 277, 267, ▧, 247, 237, 227
Pattern B: 451, 551, ▧, 751, 851, 951
Each pattern is missing one number.
What number is missing from each pattern?

Step 1

Look at Pattern A.
The digit in which place changes each time?

The digit in the ___tens___ place changes each time.

The pattern rule is ___subtract 10___.

Subtract 10. Find the missing number.

The missing number is ___257___.

> **Remember!**
> A number pattern shows numbers arranged according to a rule.

Step 2

Look at Pattern B.
The digit in which place changes each time?

The digit in the ___hundreds___ place changes each time.

The pattern rule is ___add 100___.

Add 100. Find the missing number.

The missing number is ___651___.

▷ The missing number in Pattern A is _____.

The missing number in Pattern B is _____.

Guided Practice

1. Add: 592 + 10 = ▤

When you add 10 to 592, the digits in both the tens and the hundreds places change.

9 tens + 1 ten = _____ tens

10 tens = _____ hundred

592 + 10 = _____

hundreds	tens	ones
5	**9**	2

hundreds	tens	ones
6	**0**	2

---

2. Subtract: 407 − 10 = ▤

When you subtract 10 from 407, the digits in both the tens and the hundreds places change.

407 = 4 hundreds 7 ones

There are not enough tens to subtract,

so change 1 hundred to _____ tens.

407 = 3 hundreds _____ tens 7 ones

10 tens − 1 ten = _____ tens

407 − 10 = _____

hundreds	tens	ones
4	**0**	7

hundreds	tens	ones
3	**9**	7

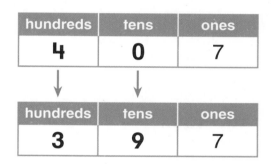

Think•Pair•Share

MP3 **3.** Otto starts at 197. He adds a number to 197 to make 207. What number does he add? How can you tell?

Independent Practice

Add 10.

1. 173 + 10 = _____

2. 215 + 10 = _____

3. 741 + 10 = _____

4. 693 + 10 = _____

Subtract 10.

5. 283 − 10 = _____

6. 486 − 10 = _____

7. 591 − 10 = _____

8. 204 − 10 = _____

Add 100.

9. 315 + 100 = _____

10. 482 + 100 = _____

11. 638 + 100 = _____

12. 195 + 100 = _____

Subtract 100.

13. 782 − 100 = _____

14. 459 − 100 = _____

15. 264 − 100 = _____

16. 158 − 100 = _____

Independent Practice

Use the number chart below for questions 17–20.

1	2	3	4	5	6	7	8	9	10
11	12	13	14	15	16	17	18	19	20
21	22	23	24	25	26	27	28	29	30
31	32	33	34	35	36	37	38	39	40
41	42	43	44	45	46	47	48	49	50
51	52	53	54	55	56	57	58	59	60
61	62	63	64	65	66	67	68	69	70
71	72	73	74	75	76	77	78	79	80
81	82	83	84	85	86	87	88	89	90
91	92	93	94	95	96	97	98	99	100

17. Start at 3. Add 10s. Circle each number as you add.

18. Start at 9. Add 10s. Draw a triangle around each number as you add.

19. Start at 95. Subtract 10s. Draw an X on each number as you subtract.

20. Start at 91. Subtract 10s. Draw a square around each number as you subtract.

Independent Practice

Add or subtract.

21. $112 + 10 =$ _____

22. $318 - 10 =$ _____

23. $828 + 10 =$ _____

24. $106 - 10 =$ _____

Circle the correct answer.

25. 100 more than 838 is _____.   848   938   948

26. 10 less than 117 is _____.   217   127   107

Solve each problem.

27. Ms. Clarkson has 325 crayons.
    Ms. Turner has 100 more crayons than Ms. Clarkson.
    How many crayons does Ms. Turner have?

    Ms. Turner has _____ crayons.

28. Diego has 286 postcards.
    Paul has 10 fewer postcards than Diego.
    How many postcards does Paul have?

    Paul has _____ postcards.

MP1 **29.** Demi wrote the two addition patterns below.
How did she add for each pattern?
Talk about how you know.

Pattern A: 485, 585, 685, 785, 885, 985

Pattern B: 137, 147, 157, 167, 177, 187

MP8 **30.** Timmy and Brian were both asked to subtract
100 from 472. Timmy says the answer is 372.
Brian says the answer is 462.

Which boy is correct?
Explain your thinking.

1. **Write how many hundreds, tens, and ones. Then write the number.**

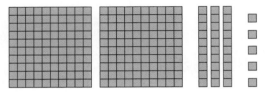

____ hundreds ____ tens ____ ones   _____

2. Skip-count by 5s.

900, _____, 910, 915, _____, _____, 930, _____, 940

3. Skip-count by 10s.

265, _____, _____, 295, _____, _____, 325, _____, 345

Write the number and the expanded form for the number name.

4. one hundred thirty-nine   _____   _____

5. six hundred eight   _____   _____

Compare. Write >, <, or =.

6. 410 ◯ 401

7. 340 ◯ 434

Add or subtract.

8.
$$\begin{array}{r} 35 \\ +44 \\ \hline \end{array}$$

9.
$$\begin{array}{r} 78 \\ -23 \\ \hline \end{array}$$

10.
$$\begin{array}{r} 92 \\ -65 \\ \hline \end{array}$$

Circle the correct answer.

11. $23 + 57 =$ ▨   70   80   710

12. $34 + 47 + 10 =$ ▨   71   83   91

13. $26 + 14 + 32 =$ ▨   62   72   76

Add or subtract.

14. $892 + 10 =$ _____

15. $115 - 100 =$ _____

Add or subtract.

16.
$$\begin{array}{r} 632 \\ +118 \\ \hline \end{array}$$

17.
$$\begin{array}{r} 457 \\ -83 \\ \hline \end{array}$$

18. Write the numbers that come next.

828, _____, _____, _____, _____, _____

MP3 19. Use the digits 5, 6, and 7 to write three different 3-digit numbers. How are your numbers alike? How are they different?

MP3 20. Kate says that she can use addition to check that her subtraction is correct. Here is Kate's work:

$$
\begin{array}{r}
\overset{4}{\cancel{5}}\ \overset{14}{\cancel{4}} \\
-\ 2\ 6 \\
\hline
2\ 8
\end{array}
\qquad
\begin{array}{r}
\overset{1}{}\ \\
2\ 8 \\
+\ 2\ 6 \\
\hline
5\ 4
\end{array}
$$

Is Kate's subtraction correct? Why can she use addition to check her subtraction?

Performance Tasks

Performance Tasks show your understanding of the math that you have learned.

Beginning This Task

This is the beginning of a Performance Task. The next three pages have problems for you to solve.

As you work, you will:

1. Show that you can use math skills and concepts

2. Decide how to solve a problem

3. Use different ways to model and solve real-world problems

Tips to help you!

- Read each problem carefully.
- Plan how you will solve the problem.
- Check your work.
- Be ready to show your work or explain your thinking.

Performance Task I

Riding the Bus

I. Alice takes the bus to school with her mom. After they got on the bus one morning, Alice counted 36 people in all on the bus.

At the first stop, 3 people got on the bus.
At the second stop, some people got off the bus.
Then there were 29 people on the bus.

a. How many people were on the bus after the first stop? Tell how you know.

b. How many people got off the bus after the second stop? Tell how you know.

Bus Station

2. At Gate A, 4 rows of are buses are parked. There are 3 buses in each row.

   At Gate B, there are 5 rows of buses with 2 buses in each row.

   a. Draw an array to show the buses parked at each gate.

   b. Write an addition equation for each array.

   Gate A: _____

   Gate B: _____

   c. How many buses are parked at Gate A and Gate B in all? Write an addition equation to help you solve the problem.

   ____ + ____ = ____

   There are ____ buses parked at Gates A and B in all.

   d. There are 17 buses parked in two rows at Gate C. Can you draw an array to show the buses parked at Gate C? Tell how you know.

Performance Task I

At the Parking Garage

3. The table shows the number of buses parked at three garages.

Garage	Number	Number Name	Expanded Form
A		two hundred ninety-nine	
B			300 + 70 + 4
C	380		

a. Complete the table by writing the missing number, number name, or expanded form.

b. Which garage has the most buses? Garage ____

c. Which garage has the fewest buses? Garage ____

d. Talk about how you found the garage with the most buses and the garage with the fewest buses.

e. How many buses in all are parked at Garage A and Garage B?

_____ buses

Progress Check

Look at how the math concepts and skills you have learned and will learn connect.

It is very important for you to understand the math concepts and skills from the prior grade level so that you will be able to develop an understanding of measurement and data in this unit and be prepared for next year. To practice your skills, go to sadlierconnect.com.

Unit **3**

GRADE 1	Before Unit 3	GRADE 2	After Unit 3	GRADE 3
I Can...		**Can I ?**		**I Will...**
Measure length in length units	☐	Use appropriate tools to measure length	☐	Measure and estimate liquid volumes and masses
	☐	Measure the length of an object with two different units	☐	
	☐	Estimate lengths in inches, feet, centimeters, and meters	☐	
Compare and order objects by length	☐	Measure to compare lengths	☐	
	☐	Solve word problems involving lengths	☐	Solve word problems involving mass or volume
	☐	Show whole numbers as lengths on a number line	☐	Solve addition and subtraction word problems about time
Tell and write time to the hour and half-hour	☐	Tell and write time to the nearest five minutes	☐	Tell and write time to the nearest minute
	☐	Solve word problems involving money	☐	
	☐	Show length measurements on a line plot	☐	Show length measurements in inches, half inches, and quarter inches on a line plot
Show data in charts and tables	☐	Draw picture and bar graphs for the same data	☐	Draw picture and bar graphs for the same data
Compare data in charts and tables	☐	Solve problems using data shown in a bar graph	☐	Use data in bar graphs to solve comparison problems

HOME◆CONNECT...

In this unit, your child will:

- Measure length in inches and feet or centimeters and meters.

- Use different units to measure length.

- Estimate, compare, add, and subtract lengths.

- Read and make number-line diagrams.

- Tell and write time to five-minute intervals.

- Solve problems involving money.

- Read and make line plots, picture graphs, and bar graphs.

Your child will learn to solve problems involving money. He or she is learning the value of coins and bills up to $10 and will be able to add money amounts, compare amounts of money, and subtract money amounts. Understanding the value of money is an important and empowering skill for children.

Your child is learning the value of the following coins and bills.

Coin or Bill	Value
Penny	1¢
Nickel	5¢
Dime	10¢
Quarter	25¢
One-dollar bill	$1
Five-dollar bill	$5
Ten-dollar bill	$10

Ways to Help Your Child

In this unit, your child will estimate the length of objects. Work with your child to estimate the length of objects in your home. Then have your child use a ruler to find the actual measurements. You might also have your child compare the length of two objects to determine which is longer or shorter. Encourage your child to estimate lengths as part of your daily routine to practice this important skill.

On the Go: The next time you are shopping with your child, choose an item in the store. Ask your child to determine if you have enough money in your wallet to purchase the item. Use the coins and bills that he or she has learned about in this unit to purchase the item.

> **ONLINE**
> **For more Home Connect activities, continue online at** sadlierconnect.com

Focus on Measurement and Data

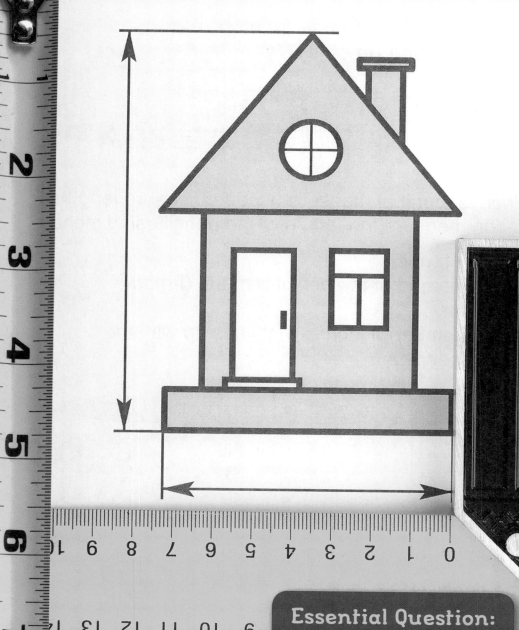

Essential Question:
How can you estimate
and measure length?

Guided Instruction

In this lesson you will learn how to measure
length using inches and feet.

Understand: **You can use an inch ruler
to find how long an object is**

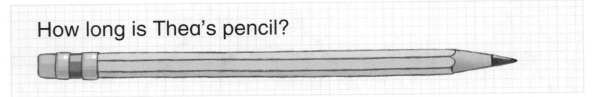

How long is Thea's pencil?

An inch is a unit of measure used to measure lengths.
You can measure the length of the pencil using inches.

Use an inch ruler.
Line up one end of the pencil with the 0-mark
on the ruler.
Find the number of inches that lines up with the
tip of the pencil.

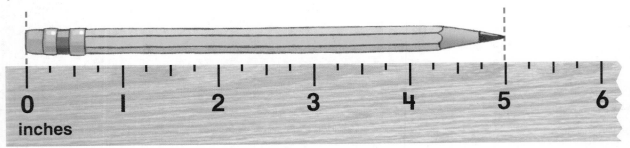

The number of inches that lines up with the tip

of the pencil is _____.

▷ Thea's pencil is 5 inches long.

Guided Instruction

Understand: You can measure objects using a yardstick or a tape measure

How long is the window in Greg's room?

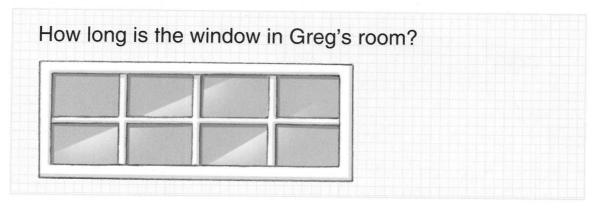

Feet and yards are units used to measure longer lengths.
One foot is the same length as 12 inches.
One yard is the same length as 36 inches, or 3 feet.

Use a yardstick or a tape measure. Line up one end with the 0-mark.

The other end lines up with the 36-inch mark, which is the same as the 3-foot mark.

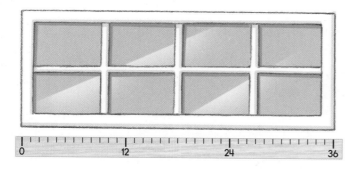

Since there are 3 feet in one yard, the window is also 1 yard long.

▷ The window in Greg's room is ____ inches,

____ feet, or ____ yard long.

Guided Practice

Connect: What you know about measuring length

How many inches long is the feather?

....

Step 1

Use an inch ruler to measure.
Line up one end of the feather with the ____-mark
on the ruler.

....

Step 2

Read the number that lines up with the other end
of the feather.

The number that lines up with the other end of the

feather is at the ____-inch mark.

⇨ The feather is ____ inches long.

Guided Practice

1. **Zarny measures the length of his TV with a tape measure.**

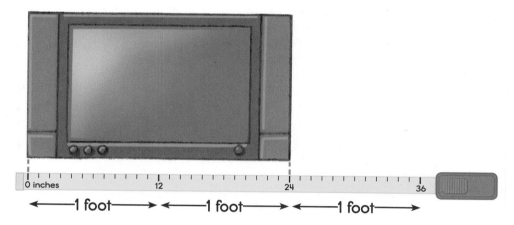

Is Zarny's TV 1 yard long?

Step 1

Zarny lines up one end of the TV with the ____-mark on the tape measure.

Step 2

The other end of the TV lines up with the ____-inch mark.

This is the same length as ____ feet.

There are 3 feet in 1 yard.

Is Zarny's TV 1 yard long? ____

MP6 **Think•Pair•Share**

2. Heather measures the length of a piece of string in inches. The string is less than 1 foot long. Which could be its length: 15 inches, 8 inches, or 12 inches? How do you know?

Independent Practice

Write the length of each object.

1.

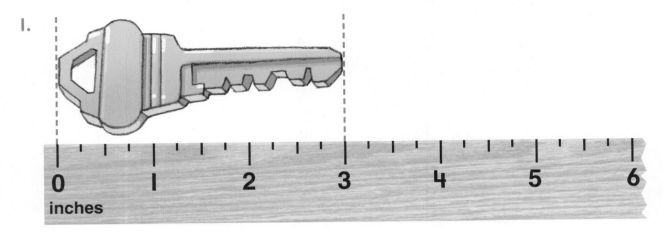

_____ inches

2.

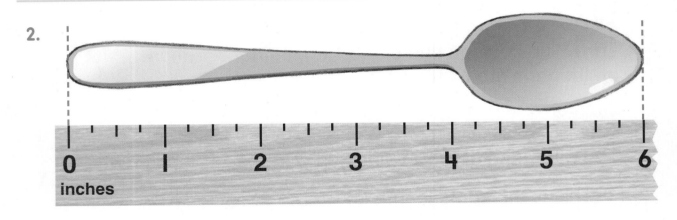

_____ inches

3.

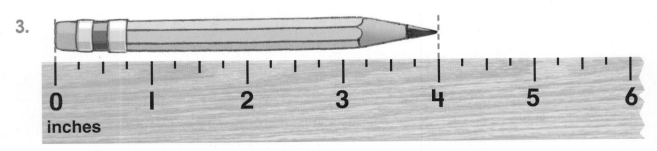

_____ inches

Independent Practice

Circle the correct answer.

4. The paintbrush is _____ long.

6 inches	7 inches	8 inches

5. The chalk is _____ long.

2 inches	3 inches	4 inches

6. The crayon is _____ long.

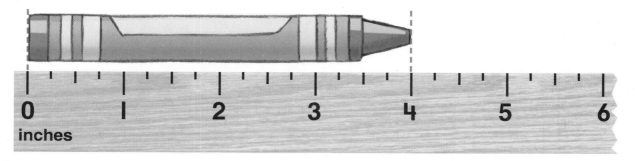

2 inches	3 inches	4 inches

Independent Practice

Use an inch ruler to measure each object.

7. How long is the toothbrush?

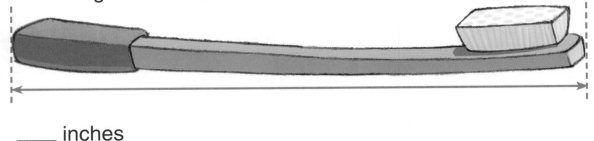

____ inches

8. How long is the comb?

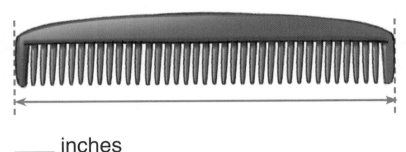

____ inches

9. How long is the marker?

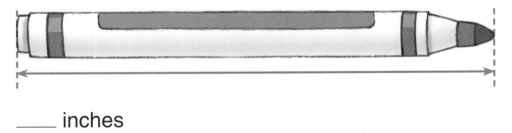

____ inches

10. Which of these might be the measure of a soccer field: 20 inches or 20 yards?

_____

Independent Practice

MP1 **11.** Aidan measures the length of a toy rocket ship.

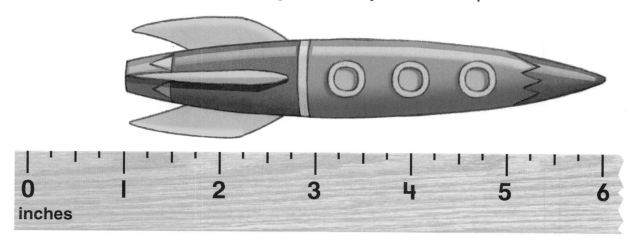

Aidan says the rocket ship is 6 inches long.
Check Aidan's work. Is he correct?
Explain your answer.

MP4 **12.** Yilda's desk is 3 feet long. She has a sheet of
poster board that is 1 foot long. She wants to
write both lengths in inches and in yards.
Can she do this? Explain.

Essential Question:
How can you measure the length of objects using centimeters or meters?

Words to Know
centimeter
meter

Guided Instruction

In this lesson you will learn how to measure length using centimeters and meters.

Understand: You can use a centimeter ruler to find how long an object is

How long is Avery's crayon?

A centimeter is a unit of measure used to measure length. You can measure the length of the crayon in centimeters.

Use a centimeter ruler.
Line up one end of the crayon with the 0-mark on the ruler.
Find the number of centimeters that lines up with the tip of the crayon.

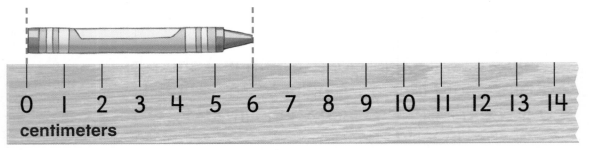

0 1 2 3 4 5 6 7 8 9 10 11 12 13 14
centimeters

Read the number of centimeters that lines up with the tip of the crayon.

➪ Avery's crayon is 6 centimeters long.

Understand: Use a meter stick to measure longer objects

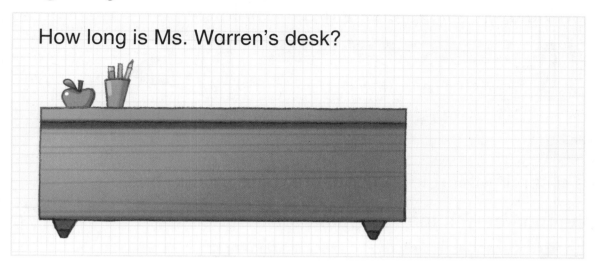

How long is Ms. Warren's desk?

A meter stick can be used to measure longer lengths. One meter is the same length as 100 centimeters.

Ms. Warren can use a meter stick to measure her desk. She lines up one end of the desk with the 0-mark on the meter stick.

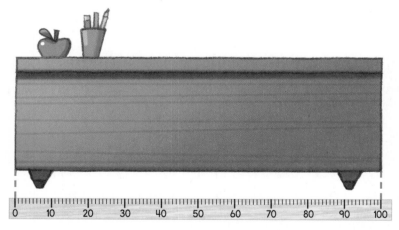

She sees that the other end of the desk lines up with the 100-centimeter mark, which is the same as the 1-meter mark.

▷ The desk is _____ centimeters long. It is _____ meter long.

Guided Practice

Connect: What you know about measuring length

How many centimeters long is the marker?

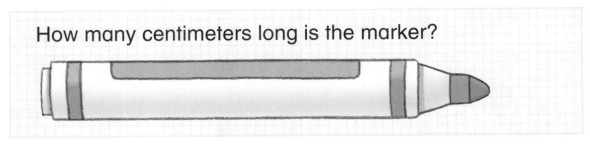

Step 1

Use a centimeter ruler to measure. Line up one end

of the marker with the _____-mark on the ruler.

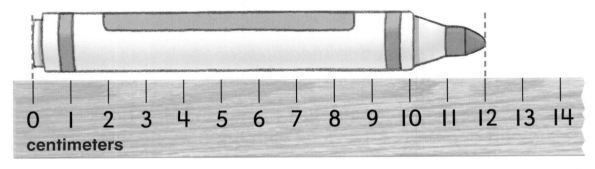

Step 2

Read the number that lines up with the tip of the marker.

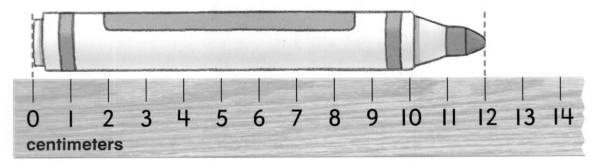

The $\underline{12}$-centimeter mark lines up with the tip
of the marker.

⇨ The marker is $\underline{12}$ centimeters long.

Guided Practice

1. **Mason uses a shovel to help his dad in the garden. He uses a meter stick to find the length of his shovel.**

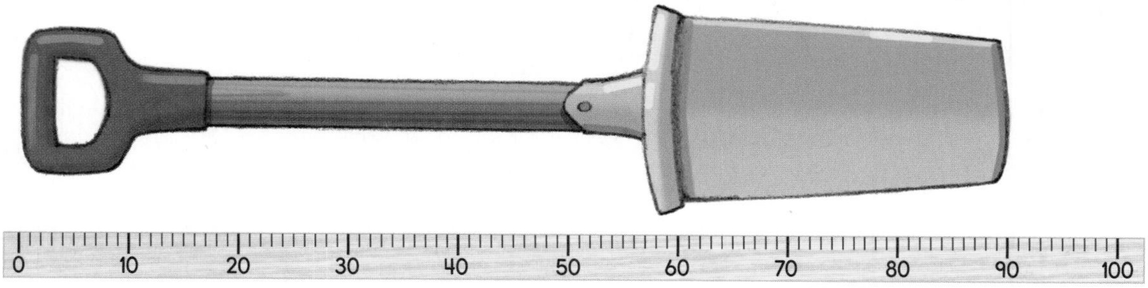

Is Mason's shovel 1 meter long?

Step 1

Mason lines up one end of the shovel with the ____-mark on the meter stick.

Step 2

He sees that the other end of the shovel lines up with

the ____-centimeter mark.

Is a length of 90 centimeters the same as a length

of 100 centimeters? ____

Is Mason's shovel 1 meter long? ____

Think•Pair•Share

MP6 2. Sariah has a kite with a long tail. She measures the tail with a meter stick. The tail is 1 meter long. Sariah says that the tail is also 200 centimeters long. Is she correct? Talk about how you know.

Independent Practice

Write the length of each object.

1.

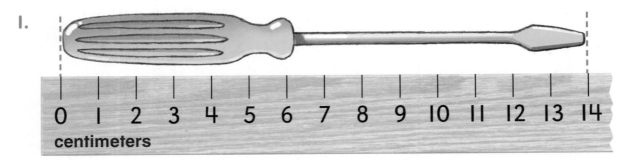

____ centimeters

2.

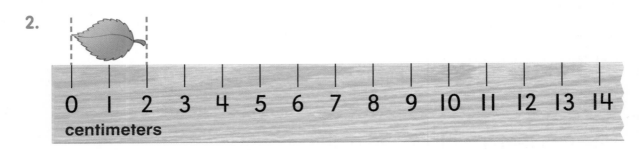

____ centimeters

3.

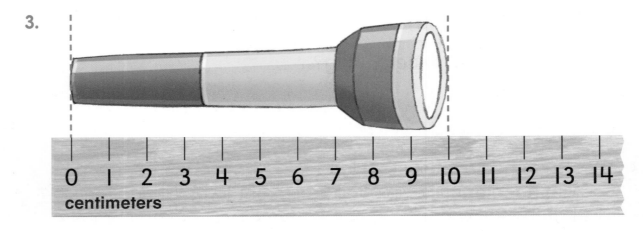

____ centimeters

Independent Practice

Circle the correct answer.

4. The wrench is _____ long.

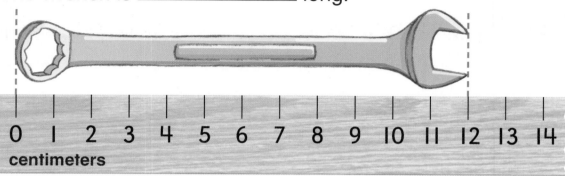

11 centimeters   12 centimeters   13 centimeters

5. The nail is _____ long.

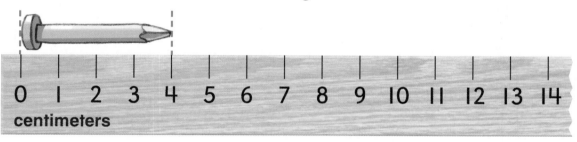

4 centimeters   5 centimeters   6 centimeters

6. The pencil is _____ long.

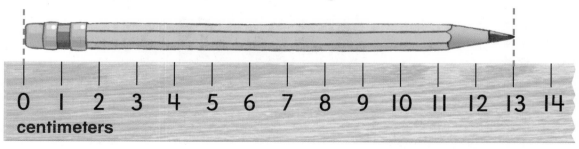

11 centimeters   12 centimeters   13 centimeters

Independent Practice

Use a centimeter ruler to measure each object.

7. How long is the straw?

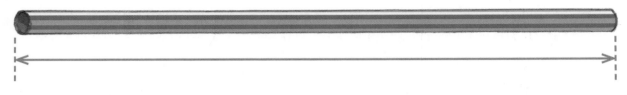

<u>15</u> centimeters

8. How long is the key?

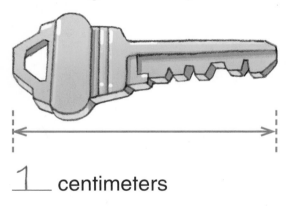

<u>1</u> centimeters

9. How long is the phone?

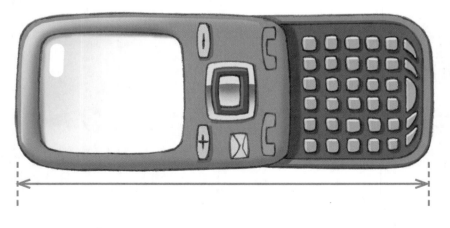

<u>11</u> centimeters

Independent Practice

MP5 **10.** Three children measure the length of the fish below. Peter says the fish is 7 centimeters long. Derrick says it is 9 centimeters long. Amy says it is 8 centimeters long.

Which child is correct? What do you think the other children did wrong? Explain.

MP1 **11.** For her project, Francisca needs a piece of yarn that is 12 centimeters long.

Yarn A

Yarn B

Yarn C

Which piece of yarn is 12 centimeters long?

_A_

Can Francisca use Yarn A for her project? Talk about your ideas.

Measure Length with Different Units

Essential Question:
How can you measure the same length with different-size units?

Guided Instruction

In this lesson you will learn how to measure the same length with different-size units.

Understand: You can use inches and feet to measure the same object

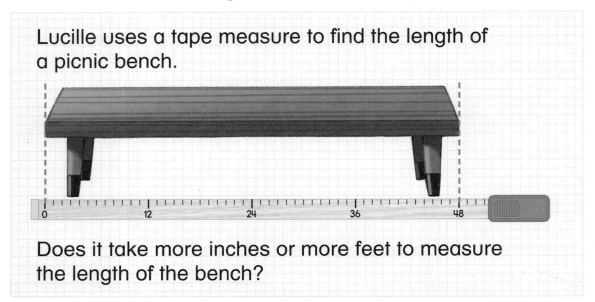

Lucille uses a tape measure to find the length of a picnic bench.

Does it take more inches or more feet to measure the length of the bench?

Lucille measured the length of the bench using inches.

The bench is 48 inches long.

Then Lucille measured the length of the bench using feet.

The bench is 4 feet long.

Inches are smaller units than feet.

▷ It takes more inches than feet to measure the bench.

Guided Instruction

Understand: You can use inches and centimeters to measure the same object

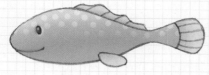

Does it take more inches or more centimeters to measure the length of this fish?

Use an inch ruler to measure the length of the fish.

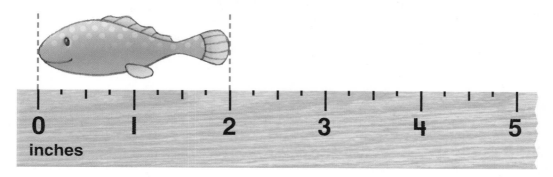

The fish is 2 inches long.

Use a centimeter ruler to measure the length of the fish.

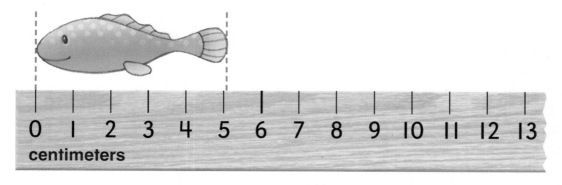

The fish is a little more than 5 centimeters long.

▷ It takes more _____ than _____ to measure the length of the fish.

Guided Instruction

Connect: **Measuring length with different-size units**

Louis has an inch ruler and Marie has a centimeter ruler. They want to know if it will take more inches or more centimeters to measure the length of a stick.

Step 1

Louis measures the length of the stick with an inch ruler.

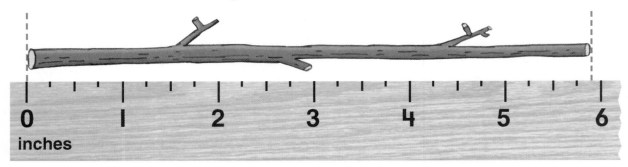

The stick is close to ___6___ inches long.

Step 2

Marie measures the length with a centimeter ruler.

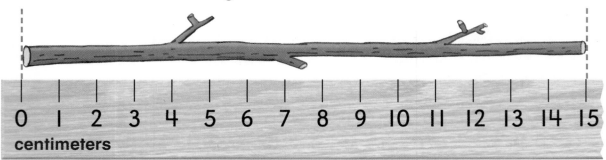

The stick is exactly ___15___ centimeters long.

▷ It takes more _____ than _____
to measure the length of the stick.

1. **Jorge measures the length of his math book in inches and in feet. Does it take more inches or more feet to measure the math book?**

Jorge measured the length using inches and feet.

1 foot

How many inches long is the book? _____

How many feet long is the book? _____

Which unit is smaller, inches or feet? _____

It takes more _____ than _____ to measure the book.

Think•Pair•Share

MP4

2. Marissa wants to measure the length of her classroom. Should she measure the length of her classroom in centimeters or in meters? Talk about why.

Independent Practice

Hyun measured the table in inches and then in feet.

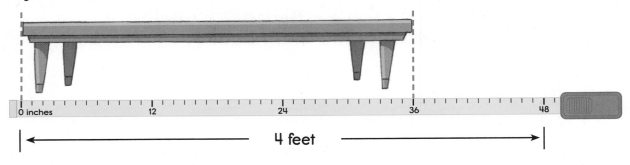

1. The table is _____ inches long.

2. The table is _____ feet long.

3. It takes more _____ than _____ to measure the length of the table.

Use an inch ruler to measure the pen. Then use a centimeter ruler to measure the pen.

4. The pen is close to _____ inches long.

5. The pen is almost _____ centimeters long.

6. It takes more _____ than _____ to measure the length of the pen.

Liam measured the window in centimeters and then in meters. He knows that 100 centimeters is equal in length to 1 meter.

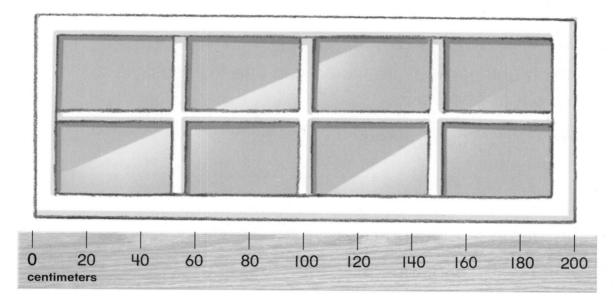

7. The window is _____ centimeters long.

8. The window is ____ meters long.

9. Which unit is smaller, centimeters or meters? _____

10. It takes more _____ than _____ to measure the length of the window.

Independent Practice

11. Which unit of measure would you use to measure the length of a soccer field?

    inches   centimeters   meters

12. Which unit of measure would you use to measure the length of a car?

    feet   centimeters   inches

13. Which unit of measure would you use to measure the length of a baseball card?

    meters   centimeters   yards

14. Do you need more inches or more centimeters to measure the length of a sandbox?

    You need more _____.

15. Do you need more feet or more yards to measure the length of a flagpole?

    You need more _____.

16. Do you need more centimeters or more feet to measure the length of a garden?

    You need more _____.

Independent Practice

MP1 17. Albert measures his violin in inches. He says that his violin is about 53 inches long. Then he measures his violin in centimeters. He says that his violin is also 21 centimeters long. What is wrong with Albert's measurements? What might he have done? Talk about it.

MP6 18. Maggie says that feet are shorter than yards. Lanie says that yards are shorter than inches. Regina says that inches are shorter than feet. Who is correct? Who is not correct? How do you know? Explain.

MP3 19. Which measurement is shorter, 15 inches or 15 centimeters? How do you know?

Essential Question:
How do you estimate the length of an object?

Words to Know
estimate

Guided Instruction

In this lesson you will learn to estimate length.

Understand: You can estimate length in inches

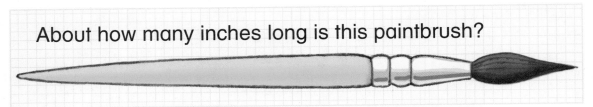

About how many inches long is this paintbrush?

Peter does not have a ruler. He can estimate the length of the paintbrush to find about how long it is.

Peter says one small paper clip is about 1 inch long. He puts paper clips under the paintbrush to estimate its length.

The paintbrush is about six 1-inch paper clips long.
Peter finds an inch ruler. He uses it to measure the paintbrush and check his estimate.

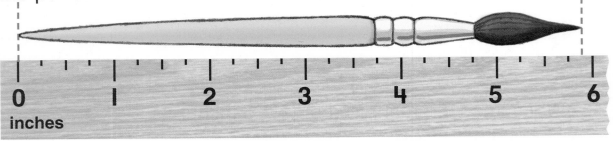

The paintbrush is almost 6 inches long.
Compare the estimate to the measured length.

▷ The paintbrush is about 6 inches long.

Understand: You can estimate length in centimeters

About how many centimeters long is this pencil?

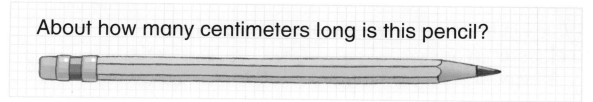

Your thumb is about 1 centimeter wide.

Think about a 1-centimeter line to help estimate.

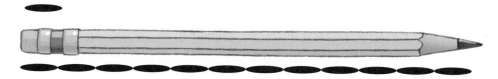

The pencil is about twelve 1-centimeter lines long.

Now measure the pencil to check your estimate.
Use a centimeter ruler.

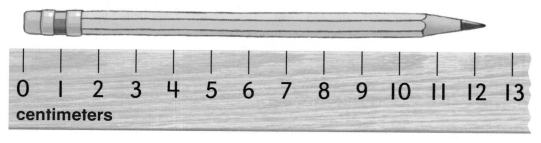

The pencil is a little more than 12 centimeters long.

Compare the estimate to the length.
The estimated length was about 12 centimeters.
The measured length was close to 12 centimeters.

▷ The pencil is about 12 centimeters long.

Guided Instruction

Connect: **What you know about estimating length**

> Which is the best estimate for the length of
> a classroom desk?
>
> 3 inches   3 centimeters   3 feet   3 meters

Step 1

Think about the size of a classroom desk.

Is a desk longer or shorter than this book? _longer_

Is a desk longer or shorter than a truck? _shorter_

Step 2

Look at each choice. Think about
the size of each unit of length.

Is 3 inches a good estimate

for the desk? _no_

　3 inches is too _short_.

Is 3 centimeters a good estimate for the desk? _no_

　3 centimeters is too _short_.

Is 3 feet a good estimate for the desk? _yes_

　3 feet is a good estimate.

Is 3 meters a good estimate for the desk? _no_

　3 meters is too _long_.

> **Remember!**
> 1 foot is the same
> 　as 12 inches.
> 1 meter is the same
> 　as 100 centimeters.

▷ The best estimate for the length of a classroom

desk is _____.

Guided Practice

1. **Estimate the length of the picture frame in inches. Then use a ruler to measure.**

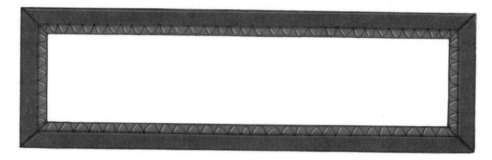

Step 1

Think about the length of an inch to help estimate. The paper clip is about 1 inch long.

The frame is about _____ paper clips long.

Step 2

Now use an inch ruler to measure the length of the frame shown above.

The frame is a little shorter than ____ inches long.

A good estimate of the length is about ____ inches.

⚐ Think•Pair•Share

MP3 2. Lilly estimates that her doll is about 6 inches tall. About how tall might her doll be in centimeters: 15 centimeters or 8 centimeters? Talk about how you chose your answer.

Independent Practice

Estimate the length of the object. Then use a ruler to measure it.

1.

   estimate: _____ inches

   measurement: _____ inches

2.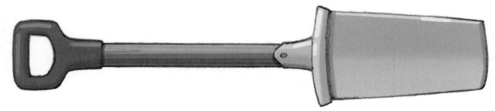

   estimate: _____ inches

   measurement: _____ inches

3.

   estimate: _____ centimeter

   measurement: _____ centimeter

4.

   estimate: _____ centimeters

   measurement: _____ centimeters

Circle the best estimate.

5. About how many inches long is this key?

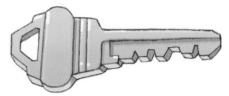

1 inch   2 inches   4 inches

6. About how many inches long is this toothpaste tube?

6 inches   4 inches   2 inches

7. About how many centimeters long is this phone?

8 centimeters   12 centimeters   15 centimeters

Independent Practice

Circle the best estimate.

8. Length of a bathtub   2 feet   4 feet   6 feet

9. Length of a desk   1 meter   3 meters   5 meters

10. Length of this book   1 foot   2 feet   3 feet

11. Length of a car   1 meter   4 meters   10 meters

Circle the correct answer.

12. Which is the best estimate for the length of a spoon?

   16 inches   16 centimeters   16 feet

13. Which is the best estimate for the length of a dollar bill?

   6 inches   6 centimeters   6 meters

14. Which is the best estimate for the length of your shoe?

   20 centimeters   20 feet   20 meters

Independent Practice

MP6 **15.** Tina and Gwen estimate the length of the playground slide. Tina thinks the slide is about 3 meters long. Gwen thinks it is about 8 meters long. They measure the slide and find that it is 350 centimeters long. Whose estimate was better? Explain your reasoning.

MP3 **16.** Use a centimeter ruler to measure the length of this crayon.

Explain how the measurement of the crayon would change if you used an inch ruler to measure it.

20 Compare Lengths

Guided Instruction

In this lesson you will learn how to compare the lengths of two objects

Understand: You can find how much longer one object is than another

How many inches longer is the green stick than the blue stick?

Line up one end of each stick with the 0-mark on an inch ruler.

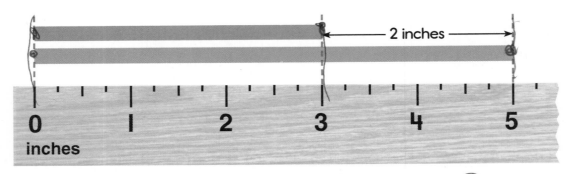

The blue stick is 3 inches long.
The green stick is 5 inches long.

Find the difference in the lengths.
5 inches − 3 inches = 2 inches

$5 - 3 = 2$
2 inches

▷ The green stick is 2 inches longer than the blue stick.

Guided Instruction

Understand: You can find how much shorter one object is than another

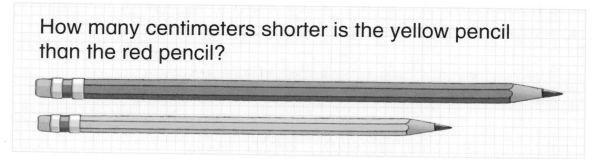

How many centimeters shorter is the yellow pencil than the red pencil?

Line up one end of each pencil with the 0-mark on a centimeter ruler.

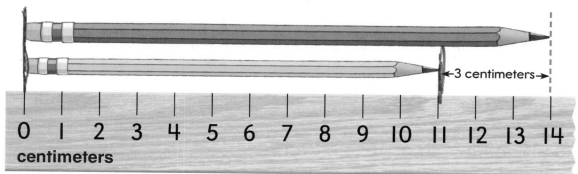

The red pencil is 14 centimeters long.
The yellow pencil is 11 centimeters long.

$3 cm$

Find the difference in the lengths.

14 centimeters − 11 centimeters = 3 centimeters

$14 - 11 = 3$

⟹ The yellow pencil is 3 centimeters shorter than the red pencil.

Guided Instruction

Connect: **What you know about comparing lengths**

Lisa and Jean each pick a carrot from the garden.
How many centimeters shorter is Jean's carrot?

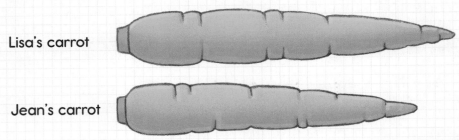

Lisa's carrot

Jean's carrot

Step 1

Line up both carrots with the ⟨0⟩-mark on a
centimeter ruler.

Step 2

Measure the length of each carrot.

Lisa's carrot

Jean's carrot

Lisa's carrot measures
__9__ centimeters long.

Jean's carrot measures
__8__ centimeters long.

```
0  1  2  3  4  5  6  7  8  9  10  11  12  13  14
centimeters
```

Subtract: 10 centimeters − 9 centimeters = __1__ centimeter

▷ Jean's carrot is __1__ centimeter shorter than Lisa's.

9 − 8 − 1 cm

Guided Practice

1. How many inches longer is the green yarn than the red yarn?

Step 1

Line up one end of each piece of yarn with the ____0____-mark on an inch ruler.

Step 2

Measure the length of each piece of yarn.

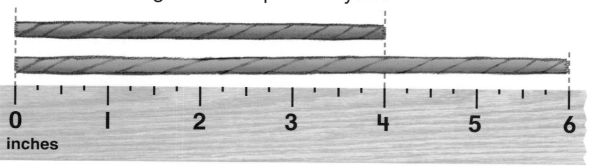

red yarn: ____ inches   green yarn: ____ inches

Subtract: ____ inches − ____ inches = ____ inches

The green yarn is ____ inches longer than the red yarn.

The red yarn is ____ inches shorter than the green yarn.

☺☺ Think•Pair•Share

MP6   **2.** Use an inch ruler. Measure the length of this book. Then measure the length of a pencil. Compare. How much longer is the book than the pencil? Measure and explain.

Independent Practice

Measure each object. Find the difference between the lengths. Write how much longer. Then write how much shorter.

1.

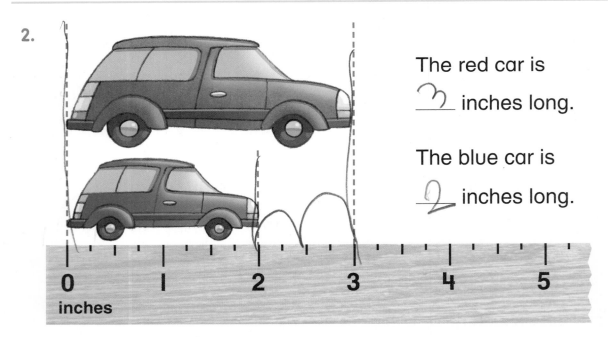

The purple strip is
5 centimeters long.

The green strip is
8 centimeters long.

The green strip is _3_ centimeters longer than the purple strip.

The purple strip is _3_ centimeters shorter than the green strip.

2.

The red car is
3 inches long.

The blue car is
2 inches long.

The red car is _1_ inch longer than the blue car.

The blue car is _1_ inch shorter than the red car.

3 − 2 = 1 inch
2 − 3 = 1 inch

Independent Practice

Measure each object. Find the difference between the lengths. Write how much longer. Then write how much shorter.

3. Use a centimeter ruler to measure the fork and the spoon.

_12_ centimeters

_8_ centimeters

The fork is _4_ centimeters longer than the spoon.

The spoon is _4_ centimeters shorter than the fork.

4. Use an inch ruler to measure the crayon and the marker.

_3_ inches

_6_ inches

The marker is _3_ inches longer than the crayon.

The crayon is _3_ inches shorter than the marker.

Independent Practice

Measure each object.
Find the difference between the lengths.

5. How many centimeters shorter is the paper clip than the feather?

The paper clip is __3__ centimeters shorter than the feather.

6. How many inches longer is the red strip than the blue strip?

blue

red

The red strip is __2__ inches longer than the blue strip.

MP3   **7.** Cindy's bracelet is 22 centimeters long. Emily's bracelet is 18 centimeters long. How many centimeters longer would Emily's bracelet need to be to make it the same length as Cindy's bracelet? Talk about your answer.

MP5   **8.** Find two objects to measure in your classroom. Draw each object below. Choose one tool to measure the length of each. Write the length of each object below its picture.

Which object is longer? How much longer? Show your work.

21 Add and Subtract Lengths

Guided Instruction

In this lesson you will learn how to add or subtract lengths to solve a problem.

Understand: You can add lengths to solve a problem

Brad has a red toy train car that is 26 centimeters long. He has a green toy train car that is 11 centimeters longer. How long is the green toy train car?

You can use a picture to help solve the problem.

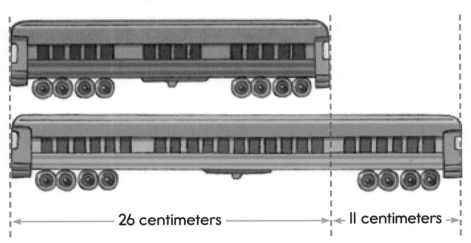

← 26 centimeters → | ← 11 centimeters →

Add to find the total length of the green toy train car.

Write an equation.

26 + 11 = ▦

Solve.
$$\begin{array}{r} 26 \\ +11 \\ \hline 37 \end{array}$$

▷ The green toy train car is 37 centimeters long.

Guided Instruction

Understand: You can subtract lengths to solve a problem

Moriah has a piece of yarn 50 centimeters long.
She cuts off a piece that is 13 centimeters long.
How much yarn does Moriah have left?

Draw a picture to show the yarn and label the parts.

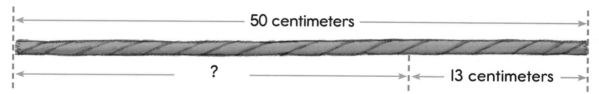

Subtract to find how much yarn Moriah has left.

Write an equation.

$$50 - 13 = \blacksquare$$

Solve.

$$
\begin{array}{r}
{}^{4}\!\!\!\not5\,{}^{10}\!\!\!\not0 \\
- 1\ 3 \\
\hline
3\ 7
\end{array}
$$

Look back at your picture to check your answer.
Is the total of 13 centimeters plus 37 centimeters
equal to 50 centimeters?

$$13 + 37 = 50$$

The total is equal to 50 centimeters.
The answer makes sense.

▷ Moriah has 37 centimeters of yarn left.

Guided Instruction

Connect: What you know about adding and subtracting lengths to solve a problem

> Connor is building a bookshelf using three boards.
> He wants the shelf to be 46 inches long.
> Board 1 is 19 inches long.
> Board 2 is 15 inches long.
> How long should Board 3 be?

Step 1

Draw a picture to model the problem.

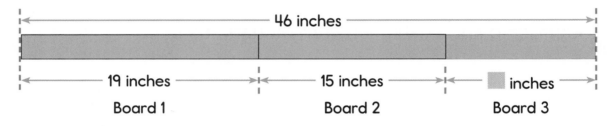

Step 2

Add to find the total length of Boards 1 and 2.

19 inches + 15 inches = ? inches

$$\begin{array}{r} 1\,9 \\ +\,1\,5 \\ \hline 3\,4 \end{array}$$

The total length of Board 1 and Board 2 is 34 inches.

Step 3

Subtract to find how long Board 3 should be.

46 inches − 34 inches = ▮ inches

$$\begin{array}{r} 4\,6 \\ -\,3\,4 \\ \hline \end{array}$$

▷ Board 3 should be _____ inches long.

1. **Mrs. Clarke's classroom is 32 feet long. Mr. Frank's classroom is 5 feet shorter than Mrs. Clarke's classroom. How long is Mr. Frank's classroom?**

Step 1

Draw a picture to show the classrooms. Label the parts.

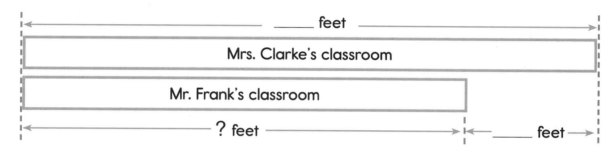

_____ feet

Mrs. Clarke's classroom

Mr. Frank's classroom

? feet   _____ feet

What do you need to find? _____

Step 2

Do you need to add or subtract to find the length? _____

Write an equation. _____ − _____ = ▢

Step 3

Solve.
$$\begin{array}{r} 3\,2 \\ -\ \ 5 \\ \hline \end{array}$$

Mr. Frank's classroom is _____ feet long.

 **Think•Pair•Share**

MP6   2. **Beth has 52 centimeters of ribbon. She uses 14 centimeters of it to make one bow and 16 centimeters of it to make another bow. How much ribbon does Beth have left? Explain.**

Independent Practice

Solve the problem. Show your work.

1. Dmitri jumped 37 inches. Then he jumped another 32 inches. How far did Dmitri jump in all?

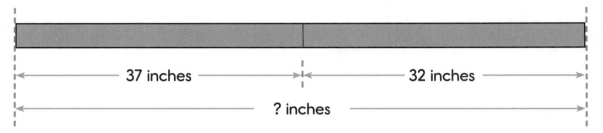

Dmitri jumped _____ inches in all.

2. Chelsea made a banner that is 43 centimeters long. Lonnie made a banner that is 16 centimeters shorter than Chelsea's. How long is Lonnie's banner?

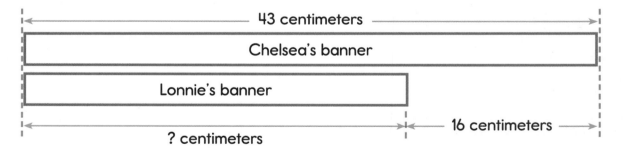

Lonnie's banner is _____ centimeters long.

Independent Practice

**Draw and label a picture for the problem.
Then write an equation to solve the problem.
Solve your equation.**

3. Sally has one string of beads that is 25 inches long.
    She has another string of beads that is 34 inches long.
    She puts the two together. How long is the string of
    beads after she puts them together?

    After she puts the two together, the string of beads

    is ____ inches long.

4. William skates 56 feet across the ice rink. The ice rink
    is 80 feet long. How much farther does William need
    to skate to get all the way across the rink?

    William needs to skate ____ more feet.

Independent Practice

Solve the problem. Show your work.

5. A roll of ribbon is 45 meters long. Mikaela cuts off a piece of the ribbon that is 9 meters long. How much ribbon is left on the roll?

   There are ____ meters of ribbon left on the roll.

6. Dominic is 42 inches tall. His father is 71 inches tall. How much taller is his father than Dominic?

   Dominic's father is ____ inches taller than Dominic.

7. The backyard fence is 36 feet long. The front yard fence is 18 feet long. A gate that is 5 feet wide joins the fences together. How long are the fences and the gate altogether?

   The fences and gate are ____ feet long altogether.

Independent Practice

MP6 **8.** Here is the path that Tommy takes when he walks from home to school. First he walks 32 meters. He turns right and walks 15 meters more. Then he turns left and walks another 20 meters. How many meters does Tommy walk to school?

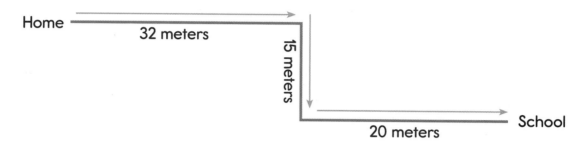

Tommy walks ＿＿＿ meters to school.

MP4 **9.** Betsy measures the lengths of two objects, a block of wood and a glue stick. The block is longer than the glue stick. One of the objects is 12 centimeters long. The sum of the two lengths is 30 centimeters. Find the length of each object. Show your work.

Essential Question:
How do you use a
number line to add
and subtract?

Words to Know
number line

Guided Instruction

In this lesson you will learn how to use
a number line to add and to subtract.

Understand: Use a number line to add

> Maya read 10 pages of a book in the library. She read
> 4 more pages at home. How many pages of the book
> did she read in all?

Use a number line to add 10 and 4. Start at 10.
To add 4, make four jumps forward.

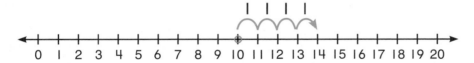

When you start at 10, and make four forward
jumps of 1, you land on 14.

$$10 + 4 = 14$$

▷ Maya read 14 pages of the book in all.

You can also show 10 + 4 with one jump.
Start at 10.
Jump forward 4.

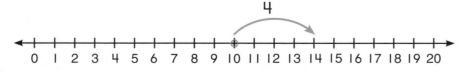

$$10 + 4 = \underline{}$$

Guided Instruction

Understand: **Use a number line to subtract**

Use a number line to find 20 − 6.

Start at 20. To subtract 6, jump back 6 from 20.

When you jump back 6 from 20, you land on ____.

▷ 20 − 6 = ____

Understand: **Use a number line with 2-digit numbers**

Use a number line to find 12 + 16.

Remember!
You can add numbers in any order.

Start with the greater addend, 16.
Break the other addend into tens and ones. 12 = 10 + 2
First add the 10. Start at 16 and jump forward 10.

When you jump forward 10 from 16, you land on 26.

Now add the 2. Start at 26 and jump forward 2.

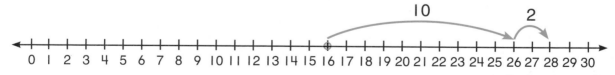

When you jump forward 2 from 26, you land on 28.

▷ 12 + 16 = 28

Guided Instruction

Connect: **What you know about number lines**

Marco has 26 stamps. He gives 18 away.
How many stamps does he have left?
Use a number line to subtract 18 from 26.

Step 1

Start at 26 on the number line.

Break 18 into tens and ones. $18 = 10 + \underline{8}$

First subtract 10. Jump back 10 from 26.

Land on 16.

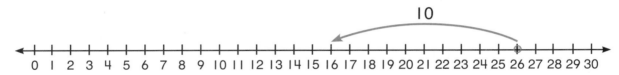

Step 2

Now subtract 8. Break 8 into 6 and 2.

Jump back 6 from 16. Land on $\underline{10}$.

Jump back 2 from 10. Land on $\underline{8}$.

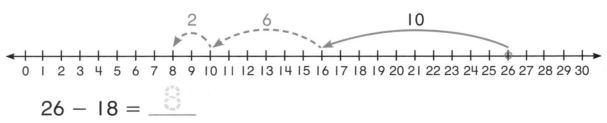

$26 - 18 = \underline{8}$

▷ Marco has ____ stamps left.

1. **Maria has 42 beads. Her sister gives her 16 more beads. How many beads does Maria have now?**

   Use a number line.

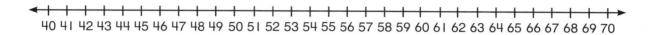

40 41 42 43 44 45 46 47 48 49 50 51 52 53 54 55 56 57 58 59 60 61 62 63 64 65 66 67 68 69 70

Step 1

Start at ____ on the number line.

Break 16 into tens and ones. 16 = 10 + ____

To add 10, jump forward ____ from ____.

Step 2

To add 6, jump forward ____ from ____.

Land on ____.

  42 + 16 = ____

Maria has ____ beads.

 **Think·Pair·Share**

MP3 2. What if Maria's sister gave her 25 beads instead of 16 beads? How would you use the number line to find 42 + 25?

Independent Practice

Add or subtract by jumping forward or back on the number line. Show your work.

1. Find $13 + 5$.

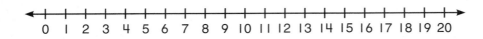

$13 + 5 =$ _____

2. Find $20 - 7$.

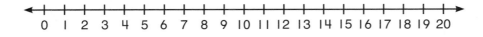

$20 - 7 =$ _____

3. Find $16 + 11$.

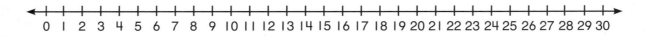

$16 + 11 =$ _____

4. Find 37 − 13. Show how you use the number line
   to find the answer.

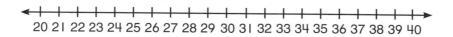

37 − 13 = _____

5. Find 17 + 13. Show how you use the number line
   to find the answer.

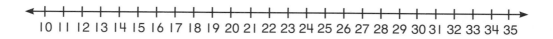

17 + 13 = _____

6. Find 24 − 12. Show how you use the number line
   to find the answer.

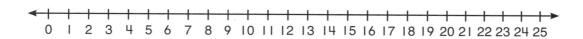

24 − 12 = _____

Independent Practice

Add or subtract using a number line to solve the problems.

7. Bailey found 21 shells. Martin found 17 shells. How many shells did they find altogether?

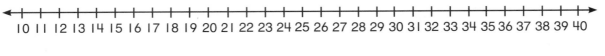

_____ shells altogether

8. Sam had a bunch of 23 grapes. He ate 12 of them. How many grapes were left?

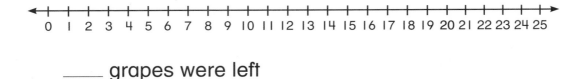

_____ grapes were left

9. Joseph has walked to school 57 days this year. Vicki has walked to school 13 days. How many more days has Joseph walked to school?

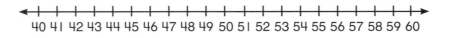

Joseph has walked to school _____ more days than Vicki.

Independent Practice

MP1 **10.** A school bus picked up 13 children at the first stop.
At the second stop, 12 more children got on the bus.
At the third stop, 14 more children got on the bus.
Then how many children in all were on the bus?

Use the number lines to find the answer.

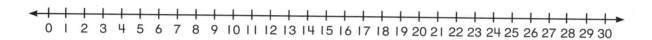

_____ children were on the bus in all.

MP6 **11.** Write numbers below the number line to complete it.
Then use the number line to find $21 - 16$.

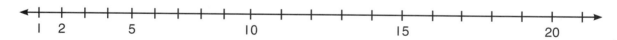

Talk about how a number line helps you find
a difference.

$21 - 16 =$ _____

Words to Know
- hour
- minute
- midnight
- noon
- A.M.
- P.M.

Guided Instruction

In this lesson you will learn how to tell time to the nearest five minutes.

Understand: Read time to the nearest five minutes

Renzo's class is on a trip to the zoo. The clock shows the time that the class gets to the zoo. What time does Renzo's class get to the zoo?

Look at the clock below. The short hand is the hour hand. The long hand is the minute hand.

The hour hand is between the 9 and the 10. This means that the time is past 9 o'clock, but not yet 10 o'clock. Look at the marks around the clock face. Each mark stands for one of the 60 minutes that make up 1 hour. There are 5 marks from each number to the next.

Start at 12. Skip count by 5s until you reach the minute hand. It is 20 minutes past 9 o'clock.
The time on the clock is 9:20.

▷ Renzo's class gets to the zoo at 9:20.

You can also show this time on a digital clock.

Understand: Read morning time and afternoon time

Natalie has soccer practice in the afternoon. The clock shows the time practice starts. What time does Natalie's soccer practice start?

Find the hour.
The hour hand is between 3 and 4. It is past 3 o'clock, but not yet 4 o'clock.

Find the minutes. Start at 12 on the clock. Skip count by 5s until you reach the minute hand.

The time on the clock is 3:45.

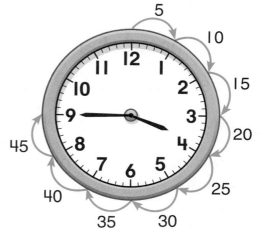

You can also show this time on a digital clock.

Midnight is 12 A.M. Noon is 12 P.M. The time from midnight to noon is A.M. time.
The time from noon until midnight is P.M. time.

Soccer practice is in the afternoon.
The afternoon is between noon and midnight.
Practice is during P.M. time.

▷ Natalie's soccer practice starts at 3:45 P.M.

Guided Instruction

Connect: What you know about telling time

The clock shows when Ethan
eats breakfast.
What time does Ethan
eat breakfast?

Step 1

Find the hour.

The hour hand is between __7__ and __8__.

It is past ____ o'clock.

Step 2

Find the minutes. Start at 12.
Skip count by 5s until you reach
the minute hand.

5, 10, ____, ____, ____, ____

It is ____ minutes past 7 o'clock.

The time is _____.

Step 3

Decide if the time is A.M. or P.M.
Do you think Ethan eats breakfast in the morning

or in the evening? _____

Is the time A.M. or P.M.? _____

▷ Ethan eats breakfast at _____

I. **The clock shows when Mr. Findlay's class eats lunch each day. What time does Mr. Findlay's class eat lunch?**

Step 1

Find the hour.

The hour hand is between ____ and ____.

It is past ____ o'clock.

Step 2

Find the minutes. Skip count by 5s.

It is ____ minutes after 12 o'clock.

The time is _____.

Step 3

Is the time A.M. or P.M.? _____

Mr. Findlay's class eats lunch at _____

Think•Pair•Share

2. The time is before noon. The hour hand on the clock is between 11 and 12 and the minute hand points to 5. What time is it? Talk about how you know the time.

Independent Practice

**Write the time for each activity.
Be sure to include A.M. or P.M.**

1. Walk the dog in the morning

8:20 a.m

2. Piano lesson in the evening

6:15 9.m

3. Leave school in the afternoon

3:05 P.m.

4. Do homework in the afternoon

4:35 p.M.

5. Wake up in the morning

6:40 a.m

6. Play ball in the park in the morning

10:50 A.m.

Draw the minute hand on the clock face to show the time on the clock above.

7.

8.

9.

10.

11.

12.

Independent Practice

Write each time. Be sure to include A.M. or P.M.

13. Lily takes her dog to the park every Saturday morning. What time do they go to the park?

_____

14. Owen has a baseball game on Thursday evening. What time is Owen's game?

_____

15. Xavier has a guitar lesson after school. What time is his guitar lesson?

_____

16. Ms. Jackson's plane lands at the airport early in the morning. What time does her plane land?

_____

Independent Practice

MP7 **17.** The clock shows the time that recess starts. Recess lasts for 15 minutes.

What time does recess start?

_____

What time does recess end?

_____

Talk about how you found the time recess ends.

MP4 **18.** What is an activity that you do about the same time every day?

Do you do this activity in the morning, afternoon, or evening?

At what time? _____

Show the time you do this activity on both clocks.

24 Money

Essential Question:
How do you solve problems with money?

Words to Know
dime
cents
penny
dollars
quarter
nickel

Guided Instruction

In this lesson you will learn how to solve problems with money.

Understand: Count on to find the total value of a group of coins

quarter 25¢	dime 10¢	nickel 5¢	penny 1¢

Rafa has these coins. How many cents does Rafa have?

A dime is worth 10 cents. Rafa has 2 dimes.

Skip-count by 10s to find how many cents 2 dimes are worth.

10¢, 20¢

A penny is worth 1 cent. Count on from 20 to find how many cents Rafa has.

10¢, 20¢, **21¢, 22¢, 23¢**

▷ Rafa has 23 cents.

Guided Instruction

Understand: **Find the value of a group of bills**

ten-dollar bill
$10

five-dollar bill
$5

one-dollar bill
$1

Jordan has three $5 bills, two $10 bills, and two $1 bills. How many dollars does Jordan have in all?

First count Jordan's bills that have the greatest value. Start with the $10 bills. Skip-count by 10s.

$10, $20

Then count the $5 bills. Start at 20 and skip-count by 5s.

$20, **$25, $30, $35**

Count on by 1s to find how many dollars Jordan has in all.

$35, **$36, $37**

⇨ Jordan has $37 in all.

Guided Instruction

Connect: What you know about finding the value of groups of bills and coins

Maria has a quarter, 3 dimes, and 2 nickels.
How many cents does Maria have in all?

Step 1

Start with the coin that has the greatest value.

One quarter is worth 25 cents.

Each dime is worth 10 cents.

Start at 25 and skip-count by 10s for the dimes.

25, **35**, **45**, **55**

Step 2

A nickel is worth 5 cents.

Start at 55 and skip-count by 5s to find how many cents Maria has in all.

55, **60**, **65**

▷ Maria has _____ cents in all.

Caleb has 1 quarter, 2 dimes, and 4 nickels.

Compare Caleb's money to Maria's money.
Does Caleb have more money, less money, or the same amount of money that Maria has?

_____

Guided Practice

I. **Jamal has 2 quarters, 2 dimes, and 2 nickels. How much money does Jamal have?**

Step I

Start with the quarters. One quarter is worth 25¢.
Find how much 2 quarters are worth.

$$25¢ + 25¢ = \blacksquare$$

$$\begin{array}{r} 2\,5\,¢ \\ +\,2\,5 \\ \hline ¢ \end{array}$$

Step 2

Count on from 50¢.
Skip-count by 10s for the dimes.

50¢, _____, _____

Now skip-count by 5s for the nickels.

70¢, _____, _____

Jamal has _____.

ᐱ†ᐱ Think•Pair•Share

2. Find different numbers of coins that make the same amount of money that Jamal has. Use at least I quarter, I dime, and I nickel.

Independent Practice

**Write the value of each group of coins.
Then draw lines to match groups with the same value.**

1.

_____ ¢

2.

_____ ¢

3.

_____ ¢

4.

_____ ¢

Write the value of each set of bills.

5. three $5 bills and
    one $10 bill

    $ _____

6. one $10 bill,
    four $5 bills, and
    one $1 bill

    $ _____

Find the amount of money.
Write $ for dollars and ¢ for cents.

7. Vicki has saved $24. Her father gives her $7 more. How many dollars does Vicki have now?

_____

8. Fred has 54¢. He buys a pencil for 15¢. How many cents does Fred have now?

_____

9. Mr. Phillips wants to buy a radio for $42. He has two $10 bills and one $5 bill. How many more dollars does Mr. Phillips need to buy the radio?

_____

10. Tatiana has 37¢. She gives 1 dime and 1 nickel to her friend. How many cents does Tatiana have now?

_____

11. Burke has 3 dimes, 4 nickels, and 3 pennies. Marta has 2 quarters, 1 nickel, and 3 pennies.

Who has more money? How much more? Fill in the blanks.

_____ has ____ more than _____.

Independent Practice

12. Mrs. Kim has two $10 bills, three $5 bills, and two
$1 bills. Find how many dollars Mrs. Kim has.

Mrs. Kim has _____ dollars.

Show a different way to make the same amount of
money as Mrs. Kim has using $10 bills, $5 bills,
and $1 bills.

13. Brian has 1 quarter, 2 dimes, a nickel, and 3 pennies.
How many cents does Brian have?

Brian has _____.

Show how to make the same amount of money as
Brian has using only dimes, nickels, and pennies.

14. Quinn has a $10 bill, three $5 bills, and seven $1 bills.
Carla has two $10 bills, three $5 bills, and two $1 bills.

Who has more money? How much more?
Fill in the blanks.

_____ has _____ more than _____.

Independent Practice

MP3 **15.** James has some quarters, dimes, and nickels worth 85¢. He spends 25¢ for an eraser.

What is the least number of coins that James could have left?

_____ coins

What are the coins that he has left? _____

Tell how you know this is the least number of coins.

MP6 **16.** Harper has two $10 bills, one $5 bill, and two $1 bills to spend on toys.

$13 $17 $11 $14

Circle the two toys she can buy using all of her money.

Tell how you chose the toys.

25 Line Plots

Essential Question:
How do you make and read a line plot?

Words to Know
line plot
data

Guided Instruction

In this lesson you will learn how to make and read a line plot that shows data.

Understand: Make a line plot

The children in Ms. Clarkson's class are growing tomato plants. They measured the height of each plant on Monday. They recorded their findings in this table.

Then the children made a line plot of the data in the table.

Heights of Tomato Plants	
Height (in inches)	**Number of Plants**
5	3
6	2
7	4
8	3

The children started the line plot by drawing a number line. They labeled it by writing the heights of the plants. They gave their line plot a title.

Then the children drew an X above the labels for the height of each plant. They drew three Xs above 5, two Xs above 6, four Xs above 7, and three Xs above 8.

▷ Here is their completed line plot.

Heights of Tomato Plants

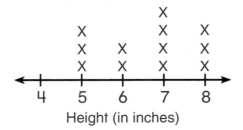

Height (in inches)

Understand: **Use a line plot**

The tally marks show the lengths of beetles in Jay's collection.

Make a line plot to show these data.

Jay's Beetle Collection	
Length (in centimeters)	Number of Beetles
1	IIII
2	HHT I
3	III
4	I
5	II
8	I

Here is the line plot.

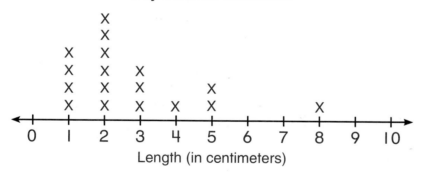

Jay's Beetle Collection

Length (in centimeters)

Use the line plot to answer this question.

How many beetles are more than 2 centimeters long?

Start at 3 on the line plot. Count the number of Xs above 3, 4, 5, and 8.

There are 7 Xs in all.

▷ Jay has _____ beetles that are more than 2 centimeters long.

Guided Instruction

Connect: What you know about making and using a line plot

Volunteers helped plant trees at a new park.

This line plot shows the heights of the trees they planted.

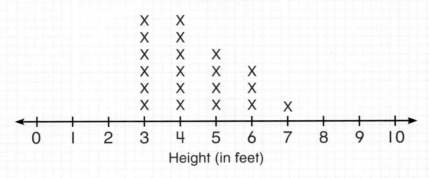

Trees Planted

Height (in feet)

How many trees did they plant that were 5 feet tall or taller?

A number line forms a scale at the bottom of the line plot.
The scale shows the height of the trees in feet.
It is marked from 0 feet to 10 feet.

Find 5 feet along the scale of the line plot.
Count the number of Xs above 5 feet.
There are 4 Xs above 5 feet.

Count the number of Xs above 6 feet.

There are _____ Xs above 6 feet.

Count the number of Xs above 7 feet. There is _____ X
above 7 feet. Add to find how many in all.

$4 + 3 + 1 =$ _____

⇨ The volunteers planted _____ trees that were
5 feet tall or taller.

1. There were 12 cars parked in a parking lot.
   Five of the cars were 3 meters long, 7 cars were
   4 meters long, and 4 cars were 5 meters long.

   Make a line plot to show these data.
   Draw Xs to complete the line plot.
   Remember to give the line plot a title.

   Title:

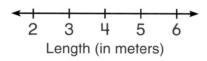

   Length (in meters)

Think•Pair•Share

MP1 2. Use the data in your line plot above to answer
   this question. One of the cars 5 meters long leaves
   the parking lot. Then 3 of the cars 4 meters long
   leave the parking lot. What length are most of the
   cars then?

   _____ meters

Independent Practice

The line plot shows the heights of the children in Mr. Wilson's class. Use the line plot to answer the questions.

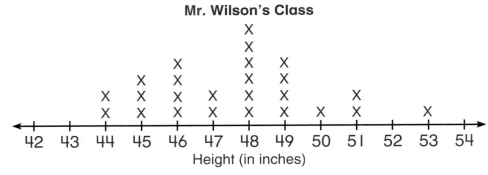

1. What height are the greatest number of children?

   _____ inches

2. How tall is the tallest child in the class?

   _____ inches

3. How many children are 46 inches tall?

   _____ children

4. How many children are 47 inches tall?

   _____ children

5. How many children are 50 or 51 inches tall?

   _____ children

6. How many children are more than 48 inches tall?

   _____ children

7. How many children are less than 46 inches tall?

   _____ children

8. How many children are in Mr. Wilson's class?

   _____ children

Independent Practice

9. James measured the length of each nail in his toolbox. He made a table to show his data. Use the number line to make a line plot of the data.

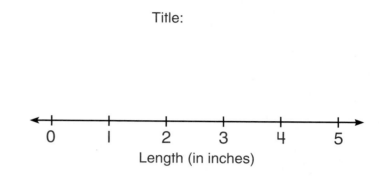

Nail Lengths	
Length (in inches)	Number of Nails
1	4
2	3
3	4
4	0
5	2

Title:

Length (in inches)

10. Emily estimated the lengths of the sharks at Ocean World. She made this line plot to show her data. Complete the table to match the data in the line plot.

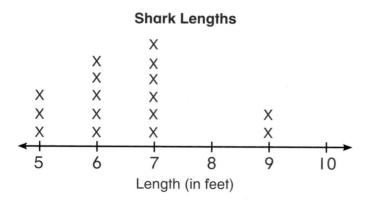

Shark Lengths

Length (in feet)

Shark Lengths	
Length (in feet)	Number of Sharks

Independent Practice

11. The table shows the lengths of some toy trucks.
Make a line plot to show the data.

Toy Truck Lengths	
Length (in inches)	Number of Trucks
2	2
3	0
4	5
5	3

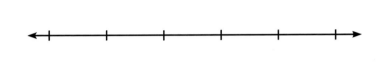

MP1 12. The lengths of some snakes in a pet store are 12, 15,
18, 12, 14, 15, 12, 14, 13, and 15 inches. Make a line
plot of these data.

Talk about how you used the numbers to make
your line plot.

Independent Practice

MP5 **13.** Janice measured the length of some crayons to the nearest centimeter (cm). She recorded the lengths in a tally chart.

Use a centimeter ruler to measure the two crayons below. Draw a tally mark in Janice's table to show each length.

Crayon Lengths	
Length (in cm)	**Number of crayons**
5	||
6	卌 |
7	卌 |
8	||
9	||

Then use the data from the table to make a line plot.

____ cm

____ cm

Talk about how your line plot helps to show the crayon data.

Essential Question:
How do you read and make a picture graph?

Words to Know
picture graph
data
key

Guided Instruction

In this lesson you will learn how to read and make picture graphs.

Understand: **Read a picture graph**

A picture graph uses pictures to show data.
A key tells what each picture stands for.
This picture graph shows the number of apples some children picked.

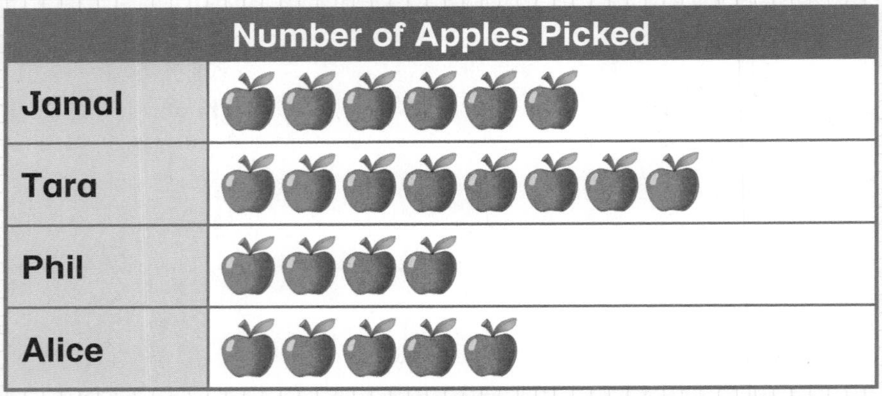

Number of Apples Picked	
Jamal	🍎🍎🍎🍎🍎🍎
Tara	🍎🍎🍎🍎🍎🍎🍎🍎
Phil	🍎🍎🍎
Alice	🍎🍎🍎🍎🍎

Key: Each 🍎 = 1 apple

How many apples did Tara pick?

Look at the graph. Find the row for Tara.
There are 8 🍎 in the row for Tara.

Look at the key below the picture graph.

The key tells you that each 🍎 stands for 1 apple.

▷ Tara picked 8 apples.

Guided Instruction

Understand: **Make a picture graph**

The table shows the number of rainy days in March, April, May, and June.

Make a picture graph to show these data.

Rainy Days	
Month	**Number of Rainy Days**
March	4
April	6
May	5
June	3

Write a title at the top of the graph.
Make a row for each month. Use a symbol to stand for a rainy day.

Write a key for your picture graph to show that each ☂ stands for 1 rainy day.

Rainy Days	
March	
April	
May	
June	

Key: Each ☂ = 1 rainy day

Fill in the picture graph.
Use 4 ☂ for the rainy days in March. Use 6 for April. Use 5 ☂ for May, and use 3 ☂ for June.

▷ This picture graph shows the data.

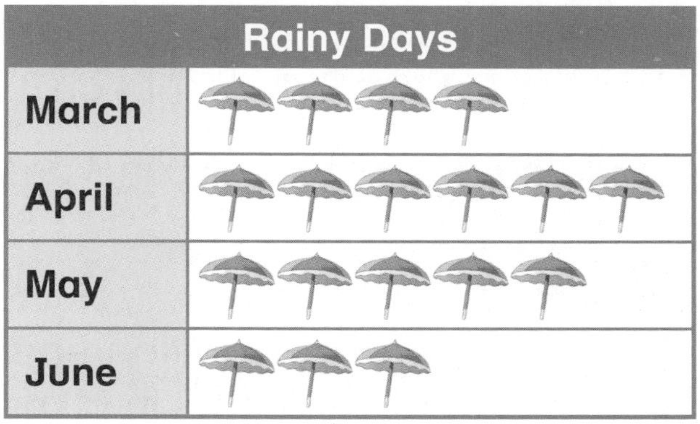

Rainy Days	
March	☂ ☂ ☂ ☂
April	☂ ☂ ☂ ☂ ☂ ☂
May	☂ ☂ ☂ ☂ ☂
June	☂ ☂ ☂

Key: Each ☂ = 1 rainy day

Guided Instruction

Connect: Use data from a picture graph to solve problems

The picture graph shows the number of tickets to the school fair that Sylvia sold on four different days.

Tickets Sylvia Sold	
Monday	TICKET TICKET TICKET TICKET
Tuesday	TICKET TICKET TICKET TICKET TICKET TICKET
Wednesday	TICKET TICKET
Thursday	TICKET TICKET TICKET

Key: Each TICKET = 1 ticket

How many tickets did Sylvia sell in all on Monday and Tuesday?

Step 1

Find the number of tickets Sylvia sold on Monday.
The key shows that each TICKET stands for 1 ticket.
Count the number of tickets she sold on Monday.
Sylvia sold 4 tickets on Monday.

Step 2

Find the tickets Sylvia sold on Tuesday. Count them.

Sylvia sold _____ tickets on Tuesday.

Step 3

Write and solve an addition equation to show how many tickets Sylvia sold in all on the two days.

$4 + 6 =$ _____

▷ Sylvia sold _____ tickets in all on Monday and Tuesday.

I. **Mrs. Ames baked bread for a bake sale. She baked 6 loaves of banana bread, 3 loaves of pumpkin bread, and 4 loaves of corn bread. Write these data in the table.**

Use the table to make a picture graph.

Loaves of Bread	
Type of Bread	**Number of Loaves**
Banana	6
Pumpkin	3
Corn	

The title of this picture graph is Loaves of Bread. The rows are labeled with types of bread.

Loaves of Bread	
Banana Bread	🍞 🍞 🍞 🍞 🍞 🍞
Pumpkin Bread	
Corn Bread	

Key: Each 🍞 = I loaf of bread

The key tells you that each 🍞 stands for I loaf of bread.

Draw bread symbols to show the numbers of loaves of pumpkin bread and corn bread.

⚇ Think•Pair•Share

MP2　2. Write a question that can be answered using the data in the Loaves of Bread picture graph.

Independent Practice

Use the picture graph to answer problems 1–6.

Thunderstorms	
June	⚡⚡⚡⚡⚡⚡
July	⚡⚡⚡⚡⚡⚡⚡
August	⚡⚡⚡⚡⚡⚡⚡⚡⚡⚡
September	⚡⚡⚡⚡⚡

Key: Each ⚡ = I use thunderstorm

1. In which month were there the most thunderstorms?

   __August__

2. In which month were there the fewest thunderstorms?

   _____

3. How many thunderstorms were there in July?

   ____ thunderstorms

4. How many thunderstorms were there in June and July altogether?

   _____ thunderstorms

5. How many more thunderstorms were there in July than September?

   _____ more thunderstorms

6. How many fewer thunderstorms were there in September than in August?

   _____ fewer thunderstorms

7. The table shows how many books some children read in a week. Use the data in the table to complete the picture graph.

Books Read	
Name	**Number of Books**
Jared	2
Deena	6
Marco	5
Tony	3

Books Read	
Jared	 📕 📕
Deena	
Marco	
Tony	

Key: Each 📕 = 1 book

8. The picture graph shows how many flowers some children picked. Use the data in the picture graph to complete the table.

Flowers Picked	
Rosa	 🌼 🌼 🌼 🌼
Erik	 🌼 🌼 🌼 🌼 🌼
Kayla	 🌼 🌼 🌼 🌼 🌼 🌼
Pedro	 🌼 🌼 🌼

Key: Each 🌼 = 1 flower

Flowers Picked	
Name	**Number of Flowers**

Independent Practice

9. The tally chart shows how many fish some friends caught.

Fish Caught	
Name	**Number of Fish Caught**
Angel	ЖЖ ЖЖ
Lauren	ЖЖ I
Parker	IIII
Ellie	ЖЖ II

Complete the picture graph to show the data in the chart.

Fishing Trip	
Angel	 🐟 🐟 🐟 🐟 🐟 🐟 🐟 🐟 🐟 🐟
Lauren	
Parker	
Ellie	

Key: Each 🐟 = I fish

Use the picture graph to answer problems 10–12.

10. Who caught the most fish?

_____

11. Who caught the fewest fish?

_____

12. Who caught more fish, Lauren or Ellie? How many more?

_____ caught _____ more fish than _____.

Independent Practice

MP2 **13.** George asked his friends to vote for their favorite color. Here are the data he collected.

red	green	blue	yellow
yellow	red	green	red
red	blue	red	blue

Complete the table to find how many votes there were for each color.

Color	Number of Votes
red	
green	
blue	
yellow	

Make a picture graph to show the data in the table.

Let 🙂 stand for 1 vote. Give your picture graph a title.

Title: _____

Color	Number of Votes
red	
green	
blue	
yellow	

Key: Each 🙂 = 1 vote

Essential Question:
How do you read and
make a bar graph?

Words to Know
bar graph

Guided Instruction

In this lesson you will learn how to read
and make bar graphs.

Understand: Read a bar graph

A bar graph uses bars to represent data.
This bar graph shows how many games
a soccer team won from April to July.

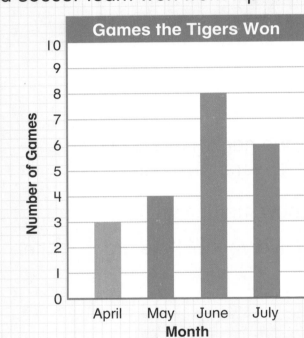

How many games did the Tigers win in May?

The scale on the left side of the graph goes from 0 to 10.

Find the bar for May. Look at the top of the bar.

Read the number on the scale that lines up with
the top of the bar.

▷ The Tigers won 4 games in May.

Understand: **Make a bar graph**

The table shows how many flowers four children picked.

Flowers Picked	
Name	**Number of Flowers**
Joey	6
Zoe	8
Anna	5
Pat	9

Make a bar graph to show these data.

The title of this bar graph is Flowers Picked.
The scale on the left side of the graph goes from 0 to 10.
The columns are labeled with the names of the children.
The bars show the number of flowers each child picked.

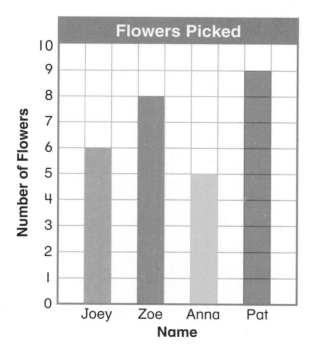

⇨ This bar graph shows the data from the table.

Guided Instruction

Connect: Use data from a bar graph to solve problems

This bar graph shows some of the pets that children in a second grade class have.

How many birds and dogs do the children have in all?

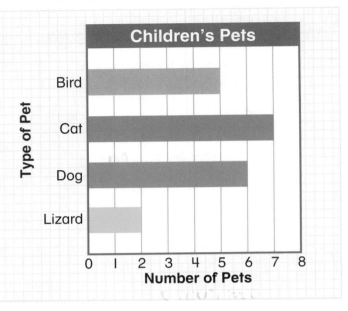

Step 1

Look at the scale below the graph.
It goes from 0 to 8 and shows the number of pets.
Find the bar for Bird. The end of the bar is above 5.
The children have 5 birds.

Step 2

Find the number of dogs the children have.
Find the bar for Dog. Look at the end of the bar.

The children have _____ dogs.

Step 3

Write and solve an addition equation
to tell how many birds and dogs in all.   5 + 6 = _____

▷ The children have _____ birds and dogs in all.

1. **Zelda picked tomatoes on four different days. She picked 5 tomatoes on Thursday, 9 tomatoes on Friday, 3 tomatoes on Saturday, and 7 tomatoes on Sunday. Write this data in the table.**

Tomatoes Picked	
Day	Number of Tomatoes Picked
Thursday	5
Friday	9
Saturday	3
Sunday	7

Use the table to make a bar graph.

The title of this bar graph is Tomatoes Zelda Picked.
The scale goes from 0 to 10.
It shows the Number of Tomatoes Picked.
The bottom of the bar graph is labeled with the Days.

Draw bars to show the data for Friday, Saturday, and Sunday.

Think•Pair•Share

MP2   2. Write a question that can be answered using the data in the Tomatoes Zelda Picked bar graph.

Independent Practice

Use this bar graph to answer problems 1–5.

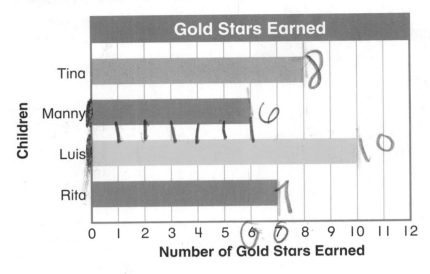

1. Who earned the fewest gold stars? __Manny__

2. How many more stars did Tina earn than Rita?

   __1__ more

3. How many gold stars did the four children earn in all?

   __31__ gold stars

4. How many fewer gold stars did Manny earn than Luis?

   __4__ fewer gold stars

5. Tina earned 2 more gold stars than her friend Sam.

   How many did Sam earn? __6__ gold stars

Independent Practice

6. The table shows the favorite fruits of some children.
Use the data in the table to complete the bar graph.
Be sure to give your graph a title.

Favorite Fruits	
Type of Fruit	**Number of Children**
Apple ✓	7
Mango ✓	6
Orange ✓	8
Peach	5

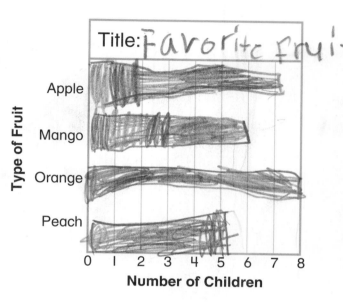

7. The bar graph shows the rainfall in Fox City from April
to July. Use the data in the bar graph to complete the table.

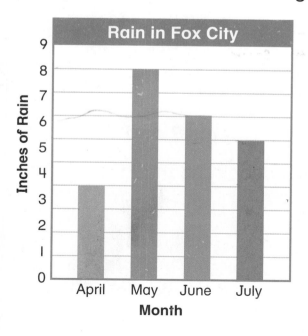

Rain in Fox City	
Month	
April	4
May	9
June	7
July	8

Independent Practice

8. The tally chart shows the number of books some children read.

Books Read	
Child	**Number of Books**
Teresa	ЖЖ IIII
Mark	ЖЖ II
Jacob	ЖЖ ЖЖ I
Flora	ЖЖ III

Complete the bar graph to match the data in the chart.

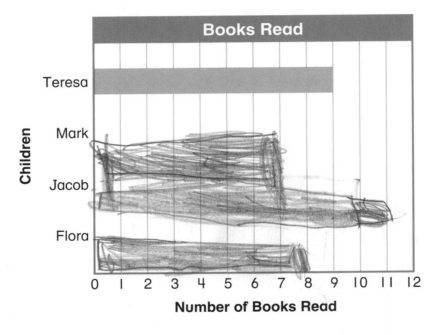

Books Read

Children

0 1 2 3 4 5 6 7 8 9 10 11 12

Number of Books Read

Use the bar graph to answer problems 9 and 10.

9. How many more books did Jacob read than Flora?

 more books

_____

10. How many books did the four children read in all?

35

Independent Practice

MP6 **11.** Use the data in the tally chart to complete the bar graph.

Tickets Sold	
Children	**Tally**
Sara	ЖЖ ЖЖ
Joe	ЖЖ |||
Alma	ЖЖ ||
Chen	ЖЖ |||

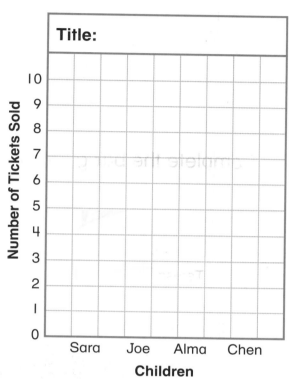

MP7 **12.** Write a question that you could answer using the data in the bar graph above. Then answer your question.

Talk about how you used the bar graph to answer your question.

1. Circle the correct answer.
   How long is the crayon?

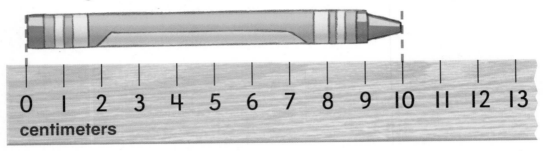

10 centimeters   11 centimeters   12 centimeters

2. Measure each object.
   How many inches longer is the blue straw
   than the orange straw?

   _____ inches

   _____ inches

   The blue straw is _____ inches
   longer than the orange straw.

3. Find 43 − 17. Show how to use the number line
   to find the answer.

   43 − 17 = _____

4. Write the time for the event. Be sure to include A.M. or P.M.

Piano lesson in the evening

_____

5. Jan used an inch ruler to measure the length of some tiles. She made a table to show her data. Use the number line to make a line plot of the data.

Tile Lengths	
Length (in inches)	Number of Tiles
1	0
2	4
3	3
4	4
5	0

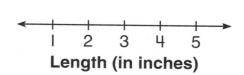

Length (in inches)

6. The table shows some children's favorite colors. Use the data in the table to complete the bar graph.

Favorite Color	
Color	Number of Children
Red	4
Blue	6
Green	3
Yellow	2

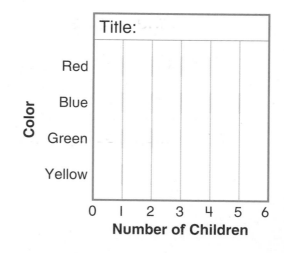

7. Do you need more inches or more yards to measure the length of a rug?

You need more _____.

8. Taylor has some quarters, dimes, and nickels worth 40¢.

What is the least number of coins Taylor could have? ____

Name the coins. _____, _____, _____

MP3 9. Use an inch ruler to measure the length of these scissors.

Explain how the measure of the scissors would change if you used a centimeter ruler to measure.

MP4 10. Niko measures the length of a toy truck and a toy tractor. The tractor is longer than the truck. One of the toys is 6 inches long. The sum of the lengths is 15 inches. Find the length of each toy. Show your work.

 **Progress Check**

 **Unit 4**

Look at how the math concepts and skills you have learned and will learn connect.

It is very important for you to understand the math concepts and skills from the prior grade level so that you will be able to develop an understanding of geometry in this unit and be prepared for next year. To practice your skills, go to sadlierconnect.com.

GRADE 1		GRADE 2		GRADE 3
I Can...	**Before Unit 4**	**Can I ?**	**After Unit 4**	**I Will...**
Understand key attributes of shapes	☐	Recognize and draw shapes with given attributes	☐	Classify quadrilaterals by their attributes
Build and draw shapes with key attributes	☐	Identify triangles, quadrilaterals, pentagons, hexagons, and cubes	☐	
		Partition a rectangle into same-size squares and count to find the total number of squares	☐	Understand area and area measurement Measure area by counting unit squares
Partition shapes into two or four equal shares	☐	Partition shapes into two, three, or four equal shares	☐	Partition shapes into parts with equal areas
Describe equal shares as halves, fourths, or quarters	☐	Describe equal shares as halves, thirds, or fourths	☐	Express the area of each equal part as a unit fraction
Describe a whole as two or four equal shares	☐	Describe a whole as two halves, three thirds, or four fourths	☐	Understand that a unit fraction names 1 of the equal parts of a whole

HOME ◆ CONNECT...

Ways to Help Your Child

In second grade and beyond, it is likely that your child will spend increasing amounts of time doing homework. Knowing the teacher's expectations for homework will allow you to help your child at home, and also gauge whether your child is spending too little or too much time completing assignments. Ask the teacher how much time he or she expects your child to spend on Math homework.

I
n second grade your child is learning to identify and draw closed, flat shapes. Your child is also identifying shapes by their numbers of sides and angles.

side ⟶ ▢ ⟵ angle

This table lists the flat shapes your child will learn to recognize and draw in this unit.

Shape	Number of sides	Number of angles
Triangle	3	3
Quadrilateral	4	4
Pentagon	5	5
Hexagon	6	6

In addition to these flat shapes, your child is learning about a solid shape called a **cube**. A cube has 6 faces. Each of the cube's faces is a square. A square is a special quadrilateral with 4 equal sides and 4 equal angles.

Activity: Ask your child to demonstrate how to partition shapes into 2, 3, and 4 equal shares. Use the terms *halves*, *thirds*, and *fourths*. Ask your child to explain how he or she knows the shares are equal.

Focus on Geometry

Essential Question:
What are halves, thirds, and fourths?

Lesson 28 — Identify and Draw Shapes

Essential Question:
How do you identify and draw shapes?

Words to Know
flat shape
sides
angles
triangle
quadrilateral
pentagon
hexagon
rectangle
square
solid shape
cube
face

Guided Instruction

In this lesson you will learn how to identify and draw shapes.

Understand: Use sides and angles to identify a flat shape

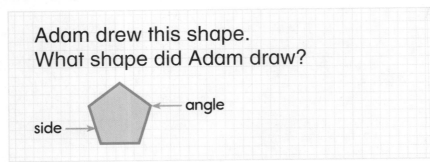

Adam drew this shape.
What shape did Adam draw?

side ⟶   ⟵ angle

You can identify a closed flat shape by its sides and its angles.

Shape		Number of Sides	Number of Angles
Triangle	△	3	3
Quadrilateral	▭	4	4
Pentagon	⬠	5	5
Hexagon	⬡	6	6

Adam's shape has 5 sides and 5 angles.

▷ Adam drew a pentagon.

Guided Instruction

Understand: Use sides and angles to identify special quadrilaterals

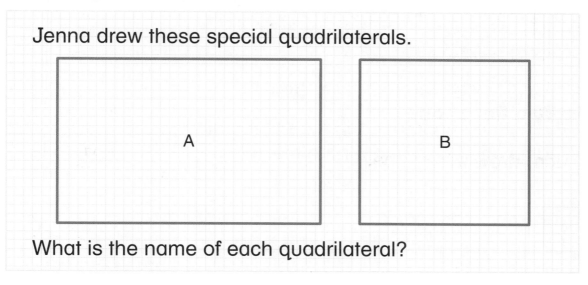

Jenna drew these special quadrilaterals.

A

B

What is the name of each quadrilateral?

You can identify each quadrilateral by comparing its sides and angles.

Look at the shapes Jenna drew.

Quadrilateral A has opposite sides that are the same length.
It has 4 angles that are the same shape.
Quadrilateral A is a rectangle.

In Quadrilateral B, all the sides are the same length.
It has 4 angles that are the same shape.
Quadrilateral B is a square.

▷ The quadrilaterals Jenna drew are a _rectangle_ and a _square_

Guided Instruction

Connect: What you know about identifying shapes

Carlos has this block.

What is the shape of each face of the block?
What is another name for the block?

Step 1

The block is a **solid shape** called a cube.

Each side of the cube is called a **face**.

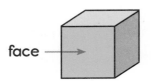

face →

Step 2

Each face of the cube is a flat shape

with ___4___ sides and ___4___ angles.

Look at one of the faces.

Are all the sides the same length? Yes

Are all the angles the same shape? Yes

Is the face a special quadrilateral? Yes

What is the name of the quadrilateral? Square

⇨ Each face of Carlos' block is a __Square__.

Another name for the block is a __Cube__.

I. **Riya drew these shapes.**
What is the name of the shapes?

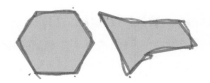

Step 1

Count the number of sides of each shape.

Do the shapes have the same number of sides? _Icg_

Count the number of angles of each shape.

Do the shapes have the same number of angles? _Yes_

Step 2

Each shape has _6_ sides and _6_ angles.

What is the name of each shape? _Hexagan_

The shapes Riya drew are _different_

Think•Pair•Share

MP2 2. Both shapes that Riya drew have the same name
but they look different.

Draw another shape with the same name
that looks different from Riya's shapes.

Talk about how you know the shapes have
the same name.

They are in the same
group Because they have 6 sides

Independent Practice

Identify the shape.
If the shape is a special quadrilateral,
write its name.

1.

triangle

2.

Quadrilateral

3.

Pentagon

4.

Quadrilateral

5.

Hexagon

6.

Square

7.

Hexagon

8.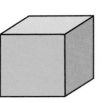

triangle

9.

Pentagon

10.

Qu rectangle

11.

cubed

12.

rectangle

Independent Practice

13. Draw a closed shape that has 5 sides. What is its name?

_____

14. Draw a closed shape that has 3 angles. What is its name?

_____

15. Draw a closed shape that has 4 angles of the same shape and 4 sides of the same length. What is its name?

_____

16. Draw a closed shape that has two pairs of opposite sides of the same length. What is its name?

_____

17. How many of the shapes you drew for problems 13–16 are quadrilaterals?

_____ shapes are quadrilaterals.

Independent Practice

18. Circle all the rectangles.

19. Circle all the triangles.

20. Circle all the quadrilaterals.

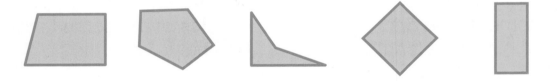

21. Circle all the hexagons.

22. Circle all the cubes.

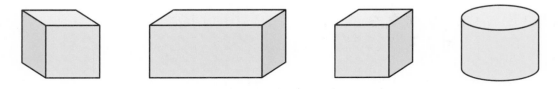

Independent Practice

MP6 **23.** Is either one of these shapes a pentagon? _____

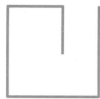

Talk about how you decided if either of the shapes
is a pentagon.

MP1 **24.** Look at this cube. What is the shape of each face

of the cube? _____

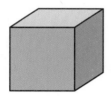

How many faces does a cube have? _____ faces

Talk about how you counted the faces.

Partition Rectangles into Same-Size Squares

Guided Instruction

In this lesson you will learn how to make same-size squares in rectangles.

Understand: **Identify rows and columns in a rectangle made up of same-size squares**

Mr. Rosa's garden is in the shape of a rectangle.
He marks his garden in same-size squares.
How many rows and columns of same-size squares are in his garden?

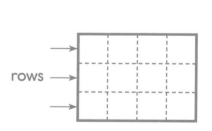

Remember!

A square is a quadrilateral with all 4 sides the same length and all 4 angles the same shape.

Count the numbers of rows and columns.

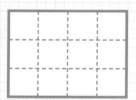

There are 3 rows.

columns

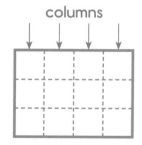

There are 4 columns.

▷ Mr. Rosa's garden has 3 rows and 4 columns of same-size squares.

Guided Instruction

Understand: Count to find the number of same-size squares in a rectangle

Find the number of same-size squares in Mr. Rosa's garden.

One way: Add the rows. There are 4 same-size squares in each row. There are three rows.

Use repeated addition to find the number of same-size squares in all three rows.

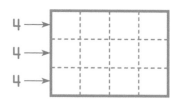

Add 4 three times: $4 + 4 + 4 = 12$

Another way: Add the columns. There are 3 same-size squares in each column. There are four columns.

Use repeated addition to find the number of same-side squares in all four columns.

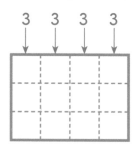

Add 3 four times: $3 + 3 + 3 + 3 = 12$

▷ There are _____ squares in Mr. Rosa's garden.

Guided Instruction

Connect: What you know about same-size squares in a rectangle

How many rows and columns of same-size squares are in this rectangle?

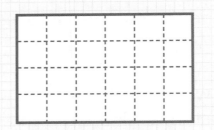

Step 1

Count the number of rows.

There are _____ rows.

Step 2

Count the number of columns.

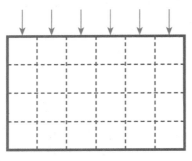

There are _____ columns.

▷ There are _____ rows and _____ columns of same-size squares in the rectangle.

Guided Practice

I. **How many same-size squares are in this rectangle?**

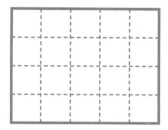

Step 1

Count the rows.

There are _____ rows of same-size squares in the rectangle.

Step 2

Count the number of same-size squares in each row.

There are _____ same-size squares in each row.

Step 3

Skip count by 5s four times.

_____, _____, _____, _____

There are _____ same-size squares in the rectangle.

Think•Pair•Share

MP3 **2.** Show how to add to find the number of same-size squares in the rectangle.

Independent Practice

How many rows and columns are in each rectangle?

1.

_____ rows

_____ columns

2.

_____ rows

_____ columns

3.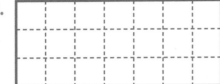

_____ rows

_____ columns

4.

_____ rows

_____ columns

Use this rectangle to answer problems 5–8.

5. How many rows?

_____ rows

6. How many columns?

_____ columns

7. How many same-size squares in each row?

_____

8. How many same-size squares in the rectangle?

_____

Independent Practice

Use this rectangle to answer problems 9–12.

9. How many rows? _____ rows

10. How many columns? _____ columns

11. How many same-size squares

    in each row? _____

12. How many same-size squares

    in the rectangle? _____

Use this rectangle to answer problems 13–15.

13. How many rows? _____ rows

14. How many same-size squares

    in each row? _____

15. How many same-size squares

    in the rectangle? _____

Use this rectangle to answer problems 16–18.

16. How many rows? _____ rows

17. How many same-size squares

    in each row? _____

18. How many same-size squares

    in the rectangle? _____

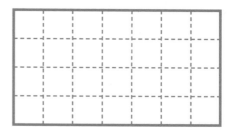

Independent Practice

Write how many same-size squares there are in each rectangle.

19.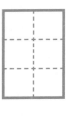

_____

20.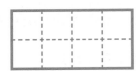

_____

21.

_____

22.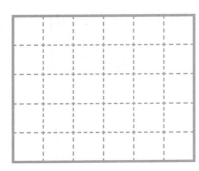

_____

23.

_____

24.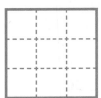

_____

Independent Practice

MP7 25. Use 18 same-size squares to draw a rectangle on this grid.

How many rows and columns are in your rectangle?

_____ rows

_____ columns

Compare your rectangle with others. What do you notice?

MP4 26. Draw a rectangle of any size on this grid.

How many rows and columns does your rectangle have?

_____ rows

_____ columns

How many same-size squares are in your rectangle?

_____ same-size squares

Essential Question:
How do you make and recognize equal shares?

Words to Know
 equal shares
 fourth
 quarter
 third
 half
 halves

Guided Instruction

In this lesson you will learn how to make and recognize equal shares.

Understand: Make equal shares of a rectangle

An artist wants to cut this rectangle into 4 equal shares.

How can she cut the rectangle to make 4 equal shares?

You can break up a whole shape into equal shares.

These drawings show two ways to break up the rectangle. Each way has 4 equal shares.

Each equal share is 1 fourth of the whole rectangle.

The whole rectangle is equal to 4 fourths.

⇨ The drawings show two ways that the artist can cut a rectangle into 4 equal shares, or 4 fourths.

A fourth is also called a quarter. Each drawing shows how the rectangle can be cut into 4 quarters.

Guided Instruction

Understand: Recognize and describe an equal share

Nick has a pita bread shaped like this circle.

How can he cut the bread into 3 equal shares?

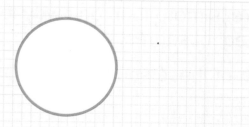

Circle A shows equal shares.

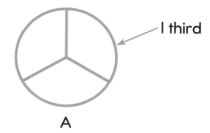

I third

A

Each share is I third of the whole.

The whole circle is equal to 3 thirds.

One of the 3 equal shares of Circle A is I third.

Circle B does not show equal shares.

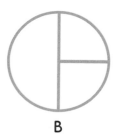

B

Circle B does not show thirds.

▷ Circle _____ shows how Nick can cut the pita bread into 3 equal shares.

Guided Instruction

Connect: **What you know about equal shares**

There is more than one way to cut a square
into equal shares.

Each of these squares is cut into equal shares.

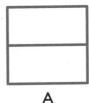
A

B

Step 1

Look at Square A.

Square A is cut into how many equal shares? _____

   Each share is 1 half of the whole.

How many halves make up the whole? _____

   There are _____ halves in the whole.

Step 2

Look at Square B.

Square B is cut into how many equal shares? _____

   Each share is _____ of the whole.

How many halves make up the whole? _____

   There are _____ halves in the whole.

The drawings show two different ways to cut a square

into _____.

I. **These rectangles are the same size. They are each cut into equal shares.**

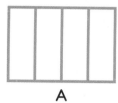

A

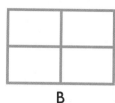

B

Step 1

Rectangle A is cut into how many equal shares? ____

Rectangle B is cut into how many equal shares? ____

Step 2

Each share of Rectangle A is what part of the whole?

_____

Each share of Rectangle B is what part of the whole?

_____

Step 3

How many fourths make up Rectangle A? _____

How many fourths make up Rectangle B? _____

Think•Pair•Share

MP5 2. Look at the equal shares in both rectangles above.

Are the equal shares the same shape? _____

Are they the same size? _____ Tell how you know.

Independent Practice

**Tell if each circle shows equal shares. Write *yes*
or *no*. If *yes*, write how many equal shares.**

1.

_____

2.

_____

3.

_____

**Tell if each quadrilateral shows equal shares.
Write *yes* or *no*. If *yes*, write how many equal shares.**

4.

_____

5.

_____

6.

_____

7.

_____

8.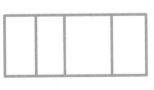

_____

9.

_____

Use this circle to answer problems 10–12.

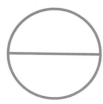

10. How many equal shares are in the circle? _____

11. What part of the circle is each equal share? _____

12. Shade 1 half of the circle.

Use this rectangle to answer problems 13–15.

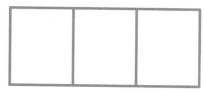

13. How many equal shares are in the rectangle? _____

14. What part of the rectangle is each equal share? _____

15. Shade 1 third of the rectangle.

16. Draw a line to make equal shares of this square. Then color one equal share.

    What part of the square did you color?

    _____

Independent Practice

**Draw lines to cut each shape into thirds.
Then color 1 third.**

17.

18.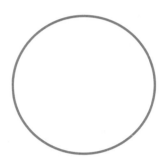

**Draw lines to cut each shape into halves.
Then color 1 half.**

19.

20.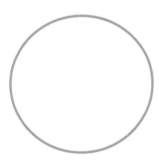

**Draw lines to cut each shape into fourths.
Then color 1 fourth.**

21.

22.

Independent Practice

MP8 **23.** These shapes are cut into equal shares.
Color one equal share of each shape.

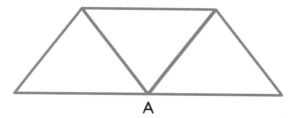 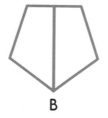 

A   B   C

Tell what part of the shape you colored.
Talk about how you know what part you colored.

MP7 **24.** Draw a line on each square to cut it into fourths.
Then color 1 fourth of each square.

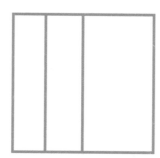  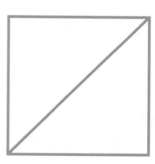

1. Draw a closed shape that has 6 sides.
   What is the name of the shape?

   Name of shape: _____

**Identify the shape. If the shape is
a special quadrilateral, write its name.**

2.

   _____

3.

   _____

4.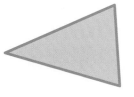

   _____

Use this rectangle to answer problems 5–7.

5. How many rows? _____

6. How many same-size squares are
   in each row? _____

7. How many same-size squares are
   in the rectangle? _____

8. Write how many same-size squares are
   in this rectangle.

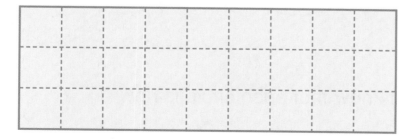

_____ same-size squares

9. Draw lines to cut the shape into thirds.
   Then color 1 third.

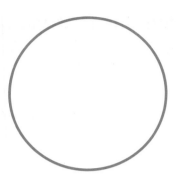

10. Draw lines to cut the shape into halves.
    Then color 1 half.

MP7 11. Draw a line to finish cutting each circle into 4 fourths
    in different ways. Color 1 fourth of each circle.

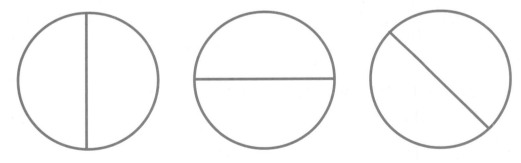

Explain how you know that each circle is now
cut into fourths.

Performance Tasks

Performance Tasks show your understanding of the math that you have learned.

Beginning This Task

This is the beginning of a Performance Task. The next three pages have problems for you to solve.

As you work, you will:

1. Show that you can use math skills and concepts

2. Decide how to solve a problem

3. Use different ways to model and solve real-world problems

Tips to help you!

- Read each problem carefully.
- Plan how you will solve the problem.
- Check your work.
- Be ready to show your work or explain your thinking.

Performance Task 2

Summer Camp

I. Every morning the children at Blue Lake Camp work on craft projects. Terry drew this fish that he planned to carve from a piece of wood.

a. Estimate the length of Terry's fish drawing in centimeters.

The drawing is about _____ centimeters long. Talk about how you estimated the length.

b. Draw a fish that you would like to carve from a piece of wood. Estimate the length of your drawing in centimeters.

c. Use a centimeter ruler to measure Terry's fish. Then measure your fish to the nearest centimeter.

Terry's fish is ____ centimeters long.

My fish is ____ centimeters long.

d. Compare the lengths. Whose fish is longer? How much longer?

_____ fish is _____ centimeters

_____ than _____ fish.

At the Camp Store

2. Keesha needs 56¢ to buy a marker.

   a. Draw coins that Keesha could use to pay for the marker.

   b. Draw a different group of coins that Keesha could use to pay for the marker.

   c. Tell how you checked the value of your groups of coins.

Performance Task 2

Blue Lake Art Project

3. Three campers collected acorns for an art project. Judy collected 13 acorns. Mia collected 8 acorns. Abel collected 11 acorns.

Camper	Acorns Collected
Judy	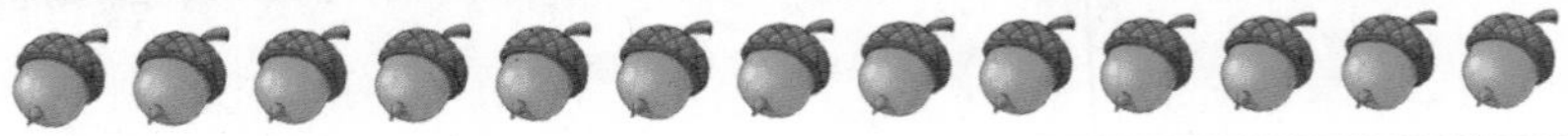
Mia	
Abel	

Key: Each 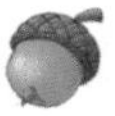 = 1 acorn

a. Complete the picture graph.

b. How many acorns did the three campers collect in all?

____ acorns

c. Make up your own questions about the data in the graph.

Addition Problems

Tyrone has 4 bananas, 3 apples, and 6 oranges.
How many fruits does he have in all?

$$4 \quad + \quad 3 \quad + \quad 6 \quad = \quad 13$$

Tyrone has 13 fruits in all.

Solve each problem.

1. Elana put 6 red marbles, 2 blue marbles, and 3 green marbles in a jar. How many marbles are in the jar?

   $6 + 2 + 3 =$ ____

   There are ____ marbles in the jar.

2. Joe has 5 green crayons and 4 blue crayons. How many crayons does he have in all?

   ____ + ____ = ____

   Joe has ____ crayons in all.

3. Ryan has 2 stickers. Julie has 6 stickers and Selene has 9 stickers. How many stickers do they have altogether?

   ____ + ____ + ____ = ____

   They have ____ stickers altogether.

Subtraction Problems

Michelle picks 8 apples.
Derrick picks 5 apples.
How many more apples did Michelle pick than Derrick?

Michelle's apples

Derrick's apples

$$8 - 5 = 3$$

Michelle picked 3 more apples than Derrick.

Solve each problem.

1. Brandon had 12 toy cars.
   He gave 5 of them to Luke.
   How many cars does
   Brandon have left?

   $12 - 5 =$ _____

   Brandon has _____ cars left.

2. Maria picks
   15 strawberries.
   Nia picks 9 strawberries.
   How many fewer
   strawberries did Nia pick
   than Maria?

   $15 - 9 =$ _____

   Nia picked _____ fewer
   strawberries than Maria.

3. Jordan's dad gives him 14 pennies. Then Jordan spent
   some of the pennies. Now he has 9 pennies left.
   How many pennies did Jordan spend?

   $14 -$ _____ $= 9$

   Jordan spent _____ pennies.

Related Facts

You can write related addition and subtraction facts using the numbers 6, 7, and 13.

$$6 + 7 = 13 \qquad\qquad 13 - 7 = 6$$
$$7 + 6 = 13 \qquad\qquad 13 - 6 = 7$$

Write the missing numbers to form related addition and subtraction facts.

1. $2 + 7 = 9$

   $9 - 7 = \underline{}$

   $7 + \underline{} = 9$

   $9 - \underline{} = 7$

2. $4 + \underline{} = 10$

   $10 - \underline{} = 4$

   $\underline{} + 4 = 10$

   $10 - 4 = \underline{}$

3. $9 + \underline{} = 12$

   $12 - \underline{} = 9$

   $3 + \underline{} = 12$

   $12 - \underline{} = 3$

4. $7 + \underline{} = 15$

   $15 - \underline{} = 7$

   $8 + 7 = \underline{}$

   $\underline{} - 7 = 8$

5. $8 + 6 = \underline{}$

   $6 + \underline{} = 14$

   $\underline{} - 6 = 8$

   $14 - \underline{} = 6$

6. $\underline{} + 9 = 16$

   $9 + \underline{} = 16$

   $\underline{} - 7 = 9$

   $16 - \underline{} = 7$

Compare Numbers

Compare 42 and 17.

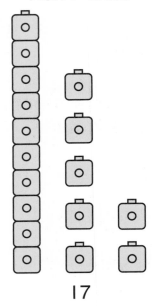

4 tens 2 ones

1 ten 7 ones

42

17

42 is greater than 17
42 > 17

17 is less than 42
17 < 42

Compare the numbers. Write >, <, or =.

1. 13 ◯ 35

2. 46 ◯ 79

3. 58 ◯ 58

4. 91 ◯ 67

5. 83 ◯ 38

6. 47 ◯ 93

7. 21 ◯ 21

8. 65 ◯ 56

Add 2-Digit Numbers

26 + 37 = ▪

Add the ones.
  6 ones + 7 ones = 13 ones
You can make a ten.
  13 ones = 1 ten 3 ones.

Add the tens.
  2 tens + 3 tens + 1 ten = 6 tens

26 + 37 = 63

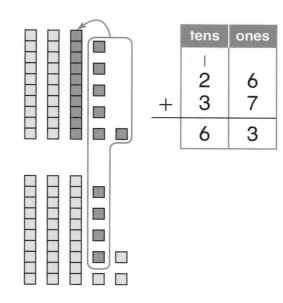

tens	ones
1	
2	6
+ 3	7
6	3

Add.

1.

tens	ones
2	4
+ 5	1

2.

tens	ones
4	8
+	3

3.

tens	ones
5	6
+ 2	8

4.

tens	ones
1	9
+ 6	0

5. 7 2
      + 1 3

6. 5 5
      +   7

Subtract Tens

$50 - 20 = $

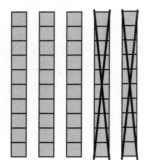

$50 = 5$ tens $20 = 2$ tens

Think of a subtraction fact that uses the tens digit of each number.

$5 - 2 = 3$

5 tens $-$ 2 tens $=$ 3 tens
3 tens $= 30$
   $50 - 20 = 30$

Subtract.

1.
$$\begin{array}{r} 2\,0 \\ -\,1\,0 \\ \hline \end{array}$$

2.
$$\begin{array}{r} 4\,0 \\ -\,3\,0 \\ \hline \end{array}$$

3.
$$\begin{array}{r} 3\,0 \\ -\,2\,0 \\ \hline \end{array}$$

4.
$$\begin{array}{r} 7\,0 \\ -\,2\,0 \\ \hline \end{array}$$

5.
$$\begin{array}{r} 5\,0 \\ -\,1\,0 \\ \hline \end{array}$$

6.
$$\begin{array}{r} 6\,0 \\ -\,4\,0 \\ \hline \end{array}$$

7.
$$\begin{array}{r} 8\,0 \\ -\,7\,0 \\ \hline \end{array}$$

8.
$$\begin{array}{r} 9\,0 \\ -\,4\,0 \\ \hline \end{array}$$

9.
$$\begin{array}{r} 4\,0 \\ +\,2\,0 \\ \hline \end{array}$$

10.
$$\begin{array}{r} 3\,0 \\ -\,3\,0 \\ \hline \end{array}$$

11.
$$\begin{array}{r} 6\,0 \\ -\,3\,0 \\ \hline \end{array}$$

12.
$$\begin{array}{r} 9\,0 \\ -\,7\,0 \\ \hline \end{array}$$

Measure Length

How long is the pencil?

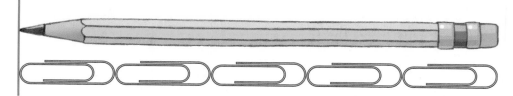

Count how many paper clips fit from one end of the pencil to the other.

The pencil is 5 paper clips long.

How long is each object?

1.

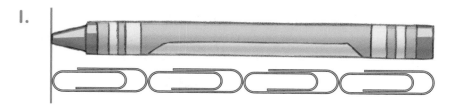

The crayon is _____ paper clips long.

2.

The feather is _____ paper clips long.

Tell Time

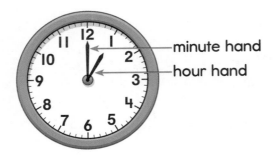

minute hand
hour hand

The hour hand points to 1.
The minute hand points to 12.
It is one o'clock.
Write 1:00.

The hour hand is
between 5 and 6.
The minute hand points to 6.
It is five thirty.
Write 5:30.

Write the time.

1.

_____ : _____

2.

_____ : _____

3.

_____ : _____

4.

_____ : _____

Tables

Look at this table.

How many votes are there for Fish?

Favorite Pet	
Kind of Pet	**Number of Votes**
Cat	4
Dog	6
Fish	2

There are 2 votes for Fish.

Use the table to answer each question.

1. How many votes are there for Cat? _____

2. Which kind of pet has the most votes? _____

3. Which kind of pet has the fewest votes? _____

4. How many more votes are there for Cat than for Fish? _____

5. How many fewer votes are there for Fish than for Dog?

    _____

6. How many votes are there in all? _____

Equal Shares

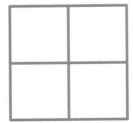

There are 2 equal parts.
2 equal parts are called
halves.

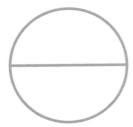

There are 4 equal parts.
4 equal parts are called
fourths, or *quarters*.

Which shapes show halves? Circle them.
Which shapes show quarters? Draw an X on them.

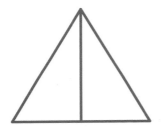

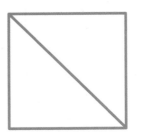

You can use this model to solve problems.

Read

Read the problem.
- What facts do you know?
- What do you need to find?

Plan

Plan how to solve the problem.
- Will you add or subtract?
- Will you draw a picture?
- Is it a one-step or a two-step problem?

Solve

Use your plan to solve the problem.
- Did you answer the question?
- Did you label your answer?

Check

Make sure your answer makes sense.
- How can you solve the problem in a different way?
- Is the answer the same?

A Fish Problem

Carlos has 15 fish.
Kim has 9 fewer fish than Carlos.
How many fish does Kim have?

What facts do you know?
Carlos: 15 fish
Kim: 9 fewer fish than Carlos has

What do you need to find?
How many fish Kim has

Plan

Carlos has more fish than Kim. He has 15 fish.
The missing number and 9 are both less than 15.
Make a drawing to show how the numbers are related.

Subtract to find the missing number.

15	
?	9

number of fish → $15 - 9 = $ ■ ← number of
Carlos has   fish Kim has

↑
9 fewer than the
number Carlos has

Solve

$15 - 9 = 6$ The missing number is 6.

➡ Kim has 6 fish.

Check

Use a related addition sentence. Start with the number
of fish Kim has. Add the number you subtracted.
The sum is the number of fish Carlos has.
$6 + 9 = 15$ The answer is correct.

A Tulip Problem

Pat has 7 tulips.
Jake has 8 more tulips than Pat.
Ana has 2 more tulips than Jake.
How many tulips does Ana have?

What facts do you know?
Pat: 7 tulips
Jake: 8 more tulips than Pat has
Ana: 2 more tulips than Jake has

What do you need to find?
How many tulips Ana has

Plan

The problem has two steps. First, add to find how many tulips Jake has.
$7 + 8 = \blacksquare$

Then add to that answer to find how many tulips Ana has.
$\blacksquare + 2 = \blacktriangle$

Solve

$7 + 8 = 15 \longrightarrow$ Jake has 15 tulips. $\longrightarrow 15 + 2 = 17$

▷ Ana has 17 tulips.

Check

Use counters to model the problem.

●●●●●●●   ●●●●●●●●   ●●
   7   +   8   = 15

15 + 2 = 17

The answer is correct.

Standards for Mathematical Practice

The Standards for Mathematical Practice, identified here, are an important part of learning mathematics. They are covered in every lesson in this book.

MP1 **Make sense of problems and persevere in solving them.**

- Analyze and plan a solution
- Relate to a similar problem
- Assess progress
- Use concrete objects or pictures
- Check solutions

MP2 **Reason abstractly and quantitatively.**

- Pay attention to all mathematical language
- Represent problems using symbols
- Consider units in problem solving
- Use properties of operations and objects

MP3 **Construct viable arguments and critique the reasoning of others.**

- Analyze a problem situation
- Share reasoning with others
- Explain an approach to a problem
- Construct arguments by using drawings or concrete objects

MP4 **Model with mathematics.**

- Relate mathematics to everyday problems
- Make assumptions and estimations
- Explain the relationship of quantities
- Use concrete tools to explain operations
- Interpret the solution in the context of a situation

MP5 **Use appropriate tools strategically.**

- Consider the range of available tools (e.g., place-value charts, graphs, clocks, etc.)
- Decide on appropriate tools to use for each situation
- Use tools carefully and strategically

MP6 **Attend to precision.**

- Communicate with precision
- Identify the meaning of symbols
- Use measurement units appropriately
- Calculate accurately
- Carefully formulate full explanations

MP7 **Look for and make use of structure.**

- Search for patterns or structure
- Evaluate the structure or design of a problem
- Discuss geometric shapes in terms of their similarities and differences

MP8 **Look for and express regularity in repeated reasoning.**

- Make generalizations in computation
- Obtain fluency using patterns
- Look for patterns with shapes and designs
- Use patterns to relate operations
- Evaluate reasonableness of answers

Key: **MP** = Mathematical Practice

292 **Standards for Mathematical Practice**

A.M. the time from midnight until noon

add to find how many in all

3 + 2 = 5

addend the numbers you add

4 + 1 = 5
↑ ↑
addends

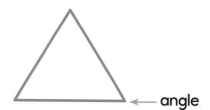

3 ← addends
+ 7 ←
1 0

angle where 2 sides meet

angle

angle

array objects arranged in equal rows and equal columns

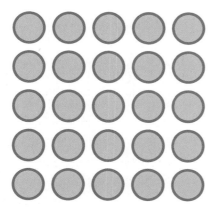

bar graph a graph that uses bars to show data

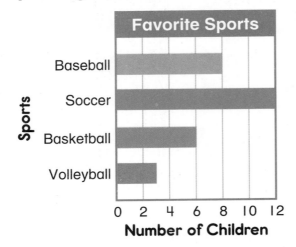

cent a unit used for money

3 cents

5 cents

centimeter a unit of measure used to measure length

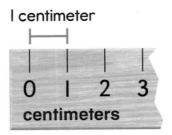

cube

294 **Glossary**

data information sometimes shown in a table or graph

Heights of Tomato Plants	
Height (in inches)	**Number of Plants**
5	3
6	2
7	4

---

difference the answer in subtraction

14 − 5 = 9
↑
difference

---

digit 0, 1, 2, 3, 4, 5, 6, 7, 8, 9 are used to write numbers

24
↑ ↑
digits

---

dime a coin worth 10 cents, or 10¢

10 cents

---

dollar a dollar is worth 100 cents, or $1

equal share

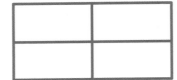 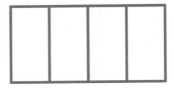

Each rectangle shows 4 equal shares.

---

equal sign (=) is equal to

$$1 + 1 = 2$$

is equal to

---

equation a number sentence with an equal sign

$$5 + 6 = 11 \qquad\qquad 8 - 6 = 2$$

---

estimate tells about how long an object is

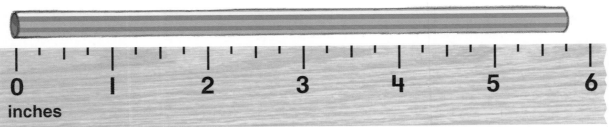

The straw is about 6 inches long.

---

even number even numbers make pairs

An even number has 0, 2, 4, 6, or 8 in the ones place.

---

expanded form

284 in expanded form is $200 + 80 + 4$

face a flat shape

face

---

flat shape

---

foot (feet) a unit of measure used to measure lengths

1 foot = 12 inches

---

fourth The rectangle is in fourths.

1 fourth, or 1 quarter, is shaded.

greater than (>) is greater than

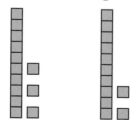

13 is greater than 12
13 > 12

half The rectangle is cut in half.

1 half is shaded.

---

halves 2 halves make a whole

2 halves are shaded. 1 whole circle is shaded.

---

hexagon a flat shape with 6 sides and 6 corners

---

hour

There are 60 minutes in 1 hour.

inch a unit of measure used to measure length

1 inch

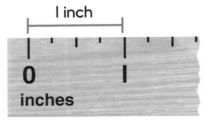

key the part of a picture graph that shows what each picture means

Books Read	
June	☐☐☐☐
July	☐☐☐☐☐☐
August	☐☐☐☐☐

Key: Each ☐ = 1 book

less than (<) is less than

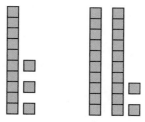

13 is less than 22
13 < 22

line plot a graph that uses a number line and Xs to show data

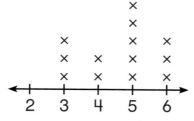

Flowers

Height (in inches)

meter a unit of measure used to measure lengths

1 meter = 100 centimeters

midnight 12 A.M.

minute There are 60 minutes in 1 hour.

nickel a coin worth 5 cents, or 5¢

5 cents

noon 12 P.M.

number line

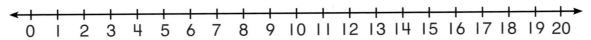

odd number odd numbers of objects make pairs
with 1 left over

An odd number has 1, 3, 5, 7, or 9 in the ones place.

P.M. the time from noon until midnight

penny a coin worth 1 cent, or 1¢

1 cent

pentagon flat shape with 5 sides and 5 angles

picture graph

Books Read	
June	☐☐☐☐
July	☐☐☐☐☐☐
August	☐☐☐☐☐

Key: Each ☐ = 1 book

place-value chart a chart that shows the value of each digit

tens	ones
6	4

64 has 6 tens and 4 ones.

quadrilateral flat shape with 4 sides and 4 angles

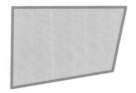

quarter a coin worth 25 cents, or 25¢

25 cents

rectangle a flat shape with 4 sides and 4 angles

regroup use 10 ones to make 1 ten or make 1 ten from 10 ones

14 ones = 1 ten 4 ones

2 tens 3 ones = 23 ones

related facts facts that have the same numbers

$$7 + 6 = 13 \qquad 13 - 6 = 7$$
$$6 + 7 = 13 \qquad 13 - 7 = 6$$

These 4 facts are related facts.

side

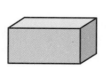

side

skip-count when you count by a number other than 1

skip-counting by 5s

  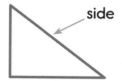

   5   10   15   20   25

solid shape

square a flat shape with 4 equal sides and 4 corners

---

subtract to find how many after taking apart, taking away from, or comparing

---

sum the answer in addition

$$4 + 3 = 7$$

sum

third The rectangle is in thirds. I third is shaded.

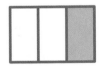

---

triangle flat shape that has 3 sides and 3 corners

yard a unit of measure used to measure lengths

One yard is the same length as 3 feet, or 36 inches.